The life of John Willi

a FORMIDABLE man

A Formidable Man © 2024 Allan Mawdsley

All Rights Reserved. No part of this book may be reproduced in any form or by any electronic or mechanical means including information storage and retrieval systems, without permission in writing from the author. The only exception is by a reviewer, who may quote short excerpts in a review.

This is a work of non-fiction. The events and conversations in this book have been set down to the best of the author's ability, although some names and details may have been changed to protect the privacy of individuals. Every effort has been made to trace or contact all copyright holders. The publishers will be pleased to make good any omissions or rectify any mistakes brought to their attention at the earliest opportunity.

Printed in Australia

Cover and internal design by Shawline Publishing Group Pty Ltd

Images in this book are copyright approved for Shawline Publishing Group Pty Ltd

First printing: June 2024

Shawline Publishing Group Pty Ltd

www.shawlinepublishing.com.au

Paperback ISBN 978-1-9231-0198-2

eBook ISBN 978-1-9231-7109-1

Hardback ISBN 978-1-9231-7121-3

Distributed by Shawline Distribution and Lightning Source Global

Shawline Publishing Group acknowledges the traditional owners of the land and pays respects to the Elders, past, present and future.

A catalogue record for this work is available from the National Library of Australia

The life of John William Springthorpe

a FORMIDABLE man

Allan Mawdsley

Contents

Illustrations	vi
Acknowledgements	ix
Foreword	xi
1. Early Years	1
2. A Prospering Career	23
3. Bereavement	47
4. Life After Annie	57
5. Springy's Textbook	84
6. Egypt	96
7. England	126
8. Home Again	142
Notes	164
Index	193

Illustrations

Figure 1: The young Dr Springthorpe	5
Figure 2: Dr John William Springthorpe	7
Figure 3: St John Ambulance Council members	9
Figure 4: Annie Inglis on her wedding day	10
Figure 5: At Warrnambool on honeymoon	11
Figure 6: 'Our first home'	12
Figure 7: Tom Roberts's portrait of Annie	92
Figure 8: Circular letter	13
Figure 9: 'What steam is to machinery…'	16
Figure 10: 'A question of medical etiquette'	17
Figure 11: 'Scene in the hall of medical infallibility'	21
Figure 12: Camelot, Collins Street, Melbourne	27
Figure 13a&b: The family at home	28
Figure 14: Cyclist Annie Springthorpe	45
Figure 15: In Memoriam – 1	49
Figure 16: In Memoriam – 2	50
Figure 17: Springthorpe Memorial (a) glass ceiling, (b) the tomb	93
Figure 18: Mackennal sculptures	94
Figure 19: Web Gilbert's 'Wheel of Life'	55
Figure 20: 'Masonmeadows'	69
Figure 21: Dr John Springthorpe KStJ	77
Figure 22: Melbourne's early motor ambulances	78
Figure 23: Joyous Gard	80
Figures 24 and 25: The old and new Melbourne Hospital	83
Figure 26: Textbook frontispiece	85
Figure 27: Textbook concluding chapter page	91
Figure 28: Mena House, No. 2 AGH.	100
Figure 29: Mena camp	100
Figure 30: Troops marching in the desert	101
Figure 31: Three glimpses of the Luna Park hospital annexe	104

Figure 32: (a) Lady Helen Munro Ferguson, (b) Colonel James Barrett, (c) Colonel Neville Howse, (d) Mr Adrian Knox. 110
Figure 33: King George V and General Monash reviewing troops 127
Figure 34: Dartford Hospital ward at Christmas 128
Figure 35: Springy's diagnostic card 136
Figure 36: (a) Dr Truby King (b) Mr Joseph Tweddle (c) Sister Maude Primrose (d) Dr Vera Scantlebury Brown 152
Figure 37: John and Daisie at Joyous Gard 154
Figure 38: Springthorpe Park gates 95
Figure 39: Springthorpe Boulevard, Macleod 95

Acknowledgements

My awareness of JWS came through my involvement in the St John Ambulance Museum. First and foremost, therefore, I must thank my St John colleagues for their primary role.

The impressive notes in the Australian Dictionary of Biography by Bryan Egan were supplemented by other notes in the Museum archival collection by Amelia Field, giving me a flying start in gathering resources. I soon made contact with Dr Jacqueline Healey, curator of the Medical History Museum at Melbourne University, who introduced me to their copy of Springy's Diary of the War 1914–1919. A year of Tuesday afternoons transcribing these barely legible entries and their handwritten marginal notes into a modern word processor gave me a vivid picture of Springy's work and personality at that phase of his life. My collaboration with Jackie on that task led to invitations to contribute notes on Springthorpe to a couple of MHM publications. I must thank Jackie for her role in convincing me that this biography warranted serious research and interpretation, not merely reporting.

Many authors have written important papers on fragments of Springy's life, but only Egan seems to have briefly surveyed the whole. It seemed clear that something more comprehensive was needed. Pat Jalland on grief, Anne Sanders on art, Peter Bladin on epilepsy, Ken Russell on the Melbourne Medical School and Harriet Edquist on the Springthorpe memorial were all significant contributors to my understanding of those issues. Other authors, like Madonna Grehan on midwifery and Anne Booth on early bicycle history, were also most helpful. Countless hours searching university archives and Trove for contemporaneous accounts of incidents filled many of the gaps. Having assembled my draft, I sought the advice of a professional manuscript editor, Belinda Nemec. I thank Belinda for her fearless highlighting of how much more had to be done to move from a story to a properly referenced biography. This help was continued by editor Aidan Demmers and the team at Shawline Publishing.

Finally, I must thank my family for their endurance and tolerance of several years of chatter about a subject that was not of their choosing but of which they are now quite knowledgeable.

Foreword

My role as honorary curator of the St John Ambulance Museum in Victoria called for some familiarity with the work of those who had gone before my own generation in this venerable society. I started to gather biographies of Knights and Dames of the Order of St John, commissioners, council members and founders of the organisation. It did not take long before John Springthorpe's name popped up in several of these categories, but we had virtually no information about him in our records.

Springthorpe was the second person in Victoria to be invested as a Knight of Grace in the Order of St John. He was also the second-longest-serving member of the St John Council in Victoria, beginning in 1886 and continuing for the next forty-five years. Annual reports gave some information about events but next to nothing about people's roles, and early council papers had not been preserved. There was very little to go on. Trying to provide a broad-ranging account of his life has been a challenging project. Nevertheless, my medical education has made the task much easier, because most of Springy's work and writing were on medical topics. His numerous other forays were not as specialised.

The hardest part of the writing has been reconciling how a man who achieved so many truly remarkable things came to have such a bleak reputation. My conclusion is that he brought it on himself. I hope this account of how his life played out will lead the reader to share the view I hold in common with Felix Meyer, whose obituary note begins the story.

Allan Mawdsley
Melbourne August 2021

1. Early Years

Independent thought and action and outspoken criticism were marked characteristics. With this independent spirit went a tenacity of purpose which made him formidable to those who did not see eye to eye with him. But his sincerity was never in question, and if at times conviction was with him the better part of argument, he convinced by the pure force of his personality where argument would have failed. Not that he was unreasonable, but he wanted things done, and he wanted them done quickly. Anything like an abuse or misuse of authority roused his fighting spirit, and having espoused a cause, he threw himself whole-heartedly into it. What is more, he got things done; he was a great driving force, with method and a full sense of detail ... He had great humanity; the pain and suffering of others touched him and moved him to action.[1]

This was John William Springthorpe, as described by his long-time friend and medical colleague Felix Meyer. Springy, as he was known, was a cultured, well-educated Victorian gentleman. Events in his life gave him many opportunities to make use of his talents and to show his fighting spirit. But his personality did not always fit well with other people's. Meyer's description was a loyal friend's way of saying that Springy was opinionated, bossy, argumentative and stubborn – but remarkably intelligent and, annoyingly, often correct.

Springthorpe was born on 29 August 1855 at Wolverhampton in Staffordshire, England, the second son of John Springthorpe (1829–1906), a mercer from Matlock in Derbyshire, and his wife, Hannah Maria Newell from Hebden Bridge in Yorkshire (1835–1906). In all, there would be thirteen children, of whom ten would live beyond the childhood years.[2] In 1860, when Springy was four, the family (which at that time had just three children) emigrated to Australia, arriving in

Sydney on the *Anglesey* in July of that year. They spent a year and a half in Melbourne before returning to Sydney, where they lived in Balmain, then a working-class area.

Young John was educated first at Fort Street Model School. This was only eleven or twelve years after the school had been established by the government, on the site of the former military hospital on Sydney's Observatory Hill, as an exemplar of how the colonial authorities wanted future schools to be run. Springy later recalled singing 'God Save the Queen' at Government House, with other children from Fort Street, to celebrate the arrival of Prince Alfred in 1868.[3] He remained there for ten years. (The school taught at both primary and secondary levels until 1911.) During this time, his siblings Florence, Amy, Albert, Edith and Charles were born.

Springy was dux of his final year at Fort Street. He then moved to Sydney Grammar School on a scholarship.[4] All three of the older sons studied at Sydney Grammar: Arthur for one year in 1868, John for three years (1869–71) and Frederick for two (1870–71).[5] The family then came back to Melbourne, where, from 1872, John completed his secondary education at Wesley College, which had been founded just six years earlier. The Springthorpe family were devout Methodists, and Wesley was doubtless chosen for this reason. Springy regularly attended church. Helping others, particularly the poor, was central to his vision of personal worth and to building the church and its missionary spirit. He shared this faith with another of his good friends at school, Edgar Inglis, whose friendship would soon prove life-changing.

At Wesley, Springy also met Felix Meyer. Meyer recalled his classmate as 'a brainy and brilliant boy, alive at every point, full of fun, impulsive, fearless, generous. Learning came easy to him.'[6] Springy was the second student to be awarded the Walter Powell Scholarship, endowed by the widow of one of the founders of Wesley College and presented to the most capable student each year, on condition that he proceed to university.

In 1874, Springy entered the University of Melbourne, studying both arts and medicine. This involved attending a double set of lectures, but he continued to excel. Despite this heavy workload, he was an active sportsman, playing football and 'fives' (a handball game played by two or four players in an enclosed court). He also enthusiastically took part in 'Hare and Hounds' (a form of cross-country footrace).[7]

He was living with his family in St Kilda at this stage, when, in the space of two months, two of his little brothers died: Frank in November 1875 at the age of five years, and Edward in January 1876 at three years. This doubtless had a destabilising effect on the family, for in 1877, when Springy was aged twenty-two and only halfway through his medical studies, his parents and younger siblings returned to England. Sadly, the family's travails did not end there: only a few months after returning to England, his sixteen-year-old sister, Amy, also died. Springy and two of his brothers, Arthur and Frederick, were left in Melbourne to be responsible for their own futures.

At this time, the Inglis family (who had grown wealthy by managing shipping and overland freight routes between Melbourne, Ballarat and Gippsland) and their circle of friends provided Springy with much-needed stability and enrichment, especially in social and cultural areas.[8] Springy often visited the family at their city house in Kew and their country property in Gippsland. He became particularly attracted to Edgar's younger sister, Annie, who was then a student at Presbyterian Ladies' College.

Annie Inglis was the sixth of nine children, and the fourth daughter (although two of her younger sisters had died in early childhood). Her father had emigrated from Fife in Scotland in around 1850 and had married a local girl, Maria Hale, in 1853. The Inglis family were cousins of the well-connected à Beckett family. Emma Minnie à Beckett was attending the National Gallery School, along with Arthur Merric Boyd (her future husband) and other future luminaries of Melbourne's art scene: Emanuel Phillips Fox, Rupert Bunny, Frederick McCubbin, Gia Follingsby, Tom Roberts, Charles Richardson and Bertram Mackennal.[9]

Springy graduated with his Bachelor of Arts in 1877, achieving first-class honours and the exhibitions in mathematics and classics, which recognised his position as top-ranking student in both classes. He then graduated with a Master of Arts in 1878, and with a Bachelor of Medicine and Surgery in 1879, again receiving first-class honours.[10] While at university, he developed his confrontational personal style with both peers and authorities. Felix Meyer described an incident where Springy acted as judge in the trial of a law student who had lampooned medical students in newspapers; Springy convicted him and sentenced him to 'involuntary immersion' (walking through the lake in front of the Student Union building). The punishment was accepted by the victim without loss of friendship.[11] Meyer also described his challenging of lecturers and heavy involvement in student politics.

One incident had serious consequences. Just after taking his third-year examinations, Springy admitted to having borrowed an important book from the library without registering it, and having passed it on to another student after using it. He was disciplined by the professorial board with the cancellation of his examination result. His appeal against the severity of the punishment revealed a conflict of authority between the university council and the professorial board, which regarded itself as responsible for student discipline. The university council ordered a reinstatement of his passing exam result.[12]

Springy was the leader of a committee appointed by the Medical Students' Society to report on the best means to secure a fairer representation in the university senate. The committee complained that the university had, by altering the requirements for senior degrees and making a new means of entry into the senate, granted facilities that favoured all existing university schools except the Medical School. The medical students contended that, as a matter of right and to place their school upon the same footing as the others, the university council should change the rules. Several mechanisms were offered for consideration, the one most favoured being creation of the degree of Master of Medicine, analogous to the existing degree of Master of Laws, which would carry that privilege.[13] This was not agreed to at the time, but was enacted some years later.

Following graduation, Springy worked for a year at Beechworth Asylum in north-east Victoria, commencing in March 1880, as acting superintendent during the absence of Dr Watkins.[14] He then left for England to undertake specialist training. He worked at a cluster of hospitals, later subsumed into the famous National Hospital for Neurology and Neurosurgery in Queen Square. This was the leading institution in neurology, where Springy undertook extramural studies, and on 27 October 1881, he became the first Australian medical graduate to be admitted to membership of the Royal College of Physicians.[15]

Springy returned from London to Australia as a ship's surgeon on the *Star of India*, arriving in Sydney on 16 November 1883, and then sailing on to Melbourne. He obtained posts as pathologist to the Alfred Hospital and assistant outpatient physician to the Melbourne Hospital, and continued his postgraduate education by obtaining the higher degree of Doctor of Medicine at the University of Melbourne in 1884. He established a private practice in Collins Street – then vying with Spring Street as Melbourne's most prestigious address for doctors – and his fortunes improved significantly. He began his important studies of patients with epilepsy, presenting the first of his papers on this subject to the Medical Society of Victoria in 1886.[16]

Figure 1: The young Dr Springthorpe

Around this time, Springy was briefly engaged to a young woman, to whom he referred in his diary only as 'Louie D'. This ended with her threatening to sue him for breach of promise, but it was settled by agreement. He afterwards referred to the relationship as 'a mistake'. He continued his involvement with the Inglis family and courted Annie. When she turned eighteen, he asked her to marry him, but was refused on the grounds that she was too young, and that he was not yet fully established in his career. He must wait.

Generally, Springy mixed with a small group of professionals and businessmen, which included solicitor and politician Theodore Fink, university lecturer and medical politician Dr James Edward Neild, professor of music G.W.L. Marshall-Hall, and scientist and anthropologist Professor Walter Baldwin Spencer. These men cultivated Melbourne's avant-garde artists, who in turn invited their patrons to smoke nights, exhibitions and studios.

Springy was also a long-standing friend of architect Harold Desbrowe-Annear, of sculptor Bertram Mackennal, and of artists Tom Roberts (who painted his portrait in 1886 and Annie's in 1887) and John Longstaff (who painted his portrait in 1895).[17] Topics of conversation included pre-Raphaelite painting and Arthurian literature – in Melbourne, Dante Gabriel Rossetti, Edward Burne-Jones and Alfred, Lord Tennyson all had their admirers, none keener than Springthorpe. It was no coincidence that Springy's principal residence was named Camelot, his later residence named Joyous Gard, and his eldest son Lancelot. The Arthurian legend resonated deeply during Victoria's reign; its courtly chivalry was the romantic metaphor of the times.[18]

A number of Springy's friends were members of the Yorick Club in Spring Street, which had begun in 1868 as informal meetings of writers held at the rooms of journalist Frederick Haddon. Among the club's early members were Marcus Clarke and his literary executor Hamilton Mackinnon, Adam Lindsay Gordon, Dr Neild, J. J. Shillinglaw and George Walstab. Members during Springy's time included Henry Kendall, George Gordon McCrae and the physician and author Patrick Moloney.

Although 'composed of gentlemen connected with literary, scientific, and artistic pursuits' the Yorick Club was initially a boisterous organisation, parodying the gentlemen's clubs of establishment

Melbourne.[19] It relocated several times in its early years because of chronic financial difficulties, due in part to membership fluctuations and irregular subscription payments. It was an early expression of the bohemian strand of the 1860s literary world but had, by the late 1880s, become more respectable.[20] Springy is said to have joined the Yorick Club around this time, and later the Melbourne-based Wallaby Club, the oldest walking club in Australia, of which he was a member from 1903 to 1929.[21]

Figure 2: Dr John William Springthorpe

He was also part of an informal group of intellectuals and artists known as 'Bohemia', who used to meet at Fasioli's, a Lonsdale Street café.[22] He joined the St John Ambulance Association Council for Victoria in 1886, just three years after its commencement, at the age of thirty-one, and would remain a member for the next forty-five years, becoming the second-longest-serving member in its history. The chairman at first was the architect Lloyd Tayler, and other members included Dr Neild and Professor Henry Martyn Andrew, one of the founding teaching staff and later headmaster of Wesley College.

It is likely that Springy was recruited by Neild, one of his university teachers and a fellow member of the Yorick Club.[23] Neild's interest in theatre and literature extended to regular contributions to magazines and newspapers as a theatre critic, and to hosting poetry and play readings at his home. In 1883, Neild had called a public meeting to garner support for the teaching of first aid in Australia. This resulted in the establishment of the Victorian branch of St John Ambulance, the first in the country. One of Melbourne's most important physicians, he was a forensic medicine specialist. He often gave evidence in court cases, and when the coroner was absent, would deputise in that role. He was deeply involved in medical politics, having been president of the Medical Society of Victoria in 1868 and continuing on its committee as editor of the *Australian Medical Journal*.

Figure 3: St John Ambulance Council members

In 1879, Neild and several like-minded colleagues formed the Victorian Branch of the British Medical Association. Ostensibly, this was to foster relationships with the profession in the 'mother country', but in actuality, it was a protest against the committee of the Medical Society of Victoria for failing to admit Dr Louis Henry to membership.

Dr Neild regarded this as an act of anti-Semitism, and declined all attempts to dissuade his resignation; the affair created a schism in local medical politics. Until this time, the Medical Society of Victoria was the only representative body for the profession in the colony. Although many doctors belonged to both organisations, some belonged to only one or the other. At the time of the schism, Springy had just graduated and was about to travel overseas; nevertheless, he was a member of both groups, though his preference lay with the British Medical Association, of which he became honorary secretary not long after his return home in November 1883.

In January 1887, the University of Melbourne confirmed Springy's appointment to a lectureship in therapeutics, dietetics and hygiene. As well as paying an annual salary of £250, the appointment was a real feather in his cap. Emboldened, he again proposed marriage to Annie. This time, he was successful. Springy was ecstatic: his dreams were coming true.

Dr John William Springthorpe and Miss Annie Constance Marie Inglis were married on 26 January 1887, which was Annie's 20th birthday. The ceremony took place at 'Eurolie', the Inglis family home at Vaucluse, part of the inner-Melbourne suburb of Richmond, with Wesleyan minister Reverend Dr James Waugh officiating.

Figure 4: Annie Inglis on her wedding day

Annie and her family were Congregationalists, and the couple subsequently attended the Congregationalist Collins Street Independent Church, nowadays called St Michael's. Their honeymoon trip involved a train journey: to Geelong, then to Camperdown, and on to Portland and Warrnambool on Victoria's south-west coast.

Figure 5: At Warrnambool on honeymoon

On their return to Melbourne on 18 February, the couple lived first in an old house at 168 Collins Street.

Figure 6: 'Our first home'

A few months later, they moved to a new house (which they named 'Camelot') at 83 Collins Street, where Springy also set up his professional rooms. The Springthorpes' first child, Dorothy Anne, was born on 6 December 1887, but died after only twenty-two days.[24] She was buried at Boroondara Cemetery in Kew.

Collecting art was an early venture of the Springthorpes'. Springy had already commissioned Tom Roberts to paint his portrait in 1886, and he commissioned one of Annie in 1887; refer to Figure 7 on page 92. (In 1891, Roberts would also paint Annie holding Enid, their second child, as a baby.[25] Springy financially supported Bertram Mackennal's travel to England, and in 1895 would commission another portrait of himself by John Longstaff.) He was secure in his hospital appointments and his private practice was thriving.

The four-yearly elections of the Melbourne Hospital's honorary medical staff were to take place in mid-1887. Springy nominated for a post as inpatient physician to replace Dr Robert Robertson, who was retiring – Springy would much prefer to be head of unit than helper. If successful, this would greatly increase his standing in the profession, and his financial prospects.

At the time, the hospital still clung to the charity hospital custom of honorary medical staff being elected by a panel of philanthropic donors. There was an unwritten law that each member of the old guard would be regularly re-elected until he chose to retire, at which time the next in line would step up to become head of unit. But Springy took the view that it should be an election of the best person for the job, and he wished to show that he was the right person. To this end, he sent a circular letter to all the Melbourne Hospital electors, in which he listed his academic and professional credentials.

There was an immediate and hostile reaction. Springy was accused of unethical behaviour by advertising.

---

168 Collins Street East, Melbourne.

To the

GOVERNORS AND SUBSCRIBERS, MELBOURNE HOSPITAL.

In support of my candidature for the vacancy on the In-Patient Staff of the MELBOURNE HOSPITAL, caused by the retirement of Dr. Robertson, I do myself the honour of inviting your consideration of the following:—

The vacancy is a legitimate one, and one to which no one has even a preferential claim.

I am a pure physician, practising medicine only, and hold by examination the highest qualifications obtainable in England as well as Victoria, viz., the M.D. of Melbourne and the M.R.C.P. of London (1881).

In addition to three years of special work in London, and numerous positions of medical responsibility, I have spent a term as Out-Patient Physician to the Hospital, having been elected in August, 1884, by the Committee (15 votes to 2). During my term of office, I have devoted on an average two hours to each visit, and been absent only on three occasions without leave. For four months also I have acted as In-Patient Physician.

In 1885, the Committee of the Alfred Hospital did me the honour of electing me as Honorary Pathologist to that institution, and the City Council of bracketing me equal with Dr. Jamieson for the Health Officership of the City.

In 1886, the University Council did me the greater honour of electing me to the new Chair of Lecturer to the Medical School in Therapeutics, Dietetics and Hygiene, out of a large field of candidates.

During the whole or portion of the last three years, I have been an active working member of the Councils of the Australian Health Society, the Convalescent Aid Society, the St. John's Ambulance Association, and the Victorian Branch of the British Medical Association, all of which have dealt with the medical aspect of public questions. I have further endeavoured to aid in the movement which aims at the re-building of the Hospital.

It is upon these grounds that I venture to claim to be a follower in the footsteps of Dr. Robertson, whose retirement is so great a loss to the institution.

Should you do me the honour of voting in my favour at the forthcoming election, I would ask you to accept my assurance that my best work will be done within the walls of the Hospital, and that, following the English practice, I shall always regard it as the patient who has first and paramount call upon my services.

I have the honour to remain,

Your most obedient Servant,

J. W. SPRINGTHORPE,
M.A., M.D., B.S., Melb.; M.R.C.P., Lond.

Figure 8: Circular letter

He was asked to appear before a special meeting of the Medical Society of Victoria. Before he could answer his critics, however, the MSV committee sent a copy of the circular to the Royal College of

Physicians in London, on the grounds that it involved an extraordinary breach of professional etiquette. Springy was furious. He fought back, using every opportunity to air his views in the public arena. The press was delighted to take up the issue:

> Dr. Springthorpe regards the action taken as unjust and injurious, and describes it as a jealous attempt to thwart his advancement by asking the opinion of one of the most Conservative bodies in England upon the conduct of one of the most democratic hospital elections in the world. It is, he says, a case of malice run mad.[26]

In a letter to the MSV, which he released to the press, Springy said that it was insulting for the MSV to have taken such action without consulting its broader membership, and that the decision had been made by a small number of the committee men, most of whom had been his rivals in various ways. He complained that the MSV had failed to inform him of the ways in which he had allegedly not followed custom or said anything unworthy or untrue. He demanded the opportunity to put his defence to a general meeting of the MSV, which responded by calling a special general meeting on 10 August, just over a week before the election was due to take place, 'to consider Dr Springthorpe's complaint against the committee'.[27]

In the lead-up to the special meeting, the war of words in the papers continued. Representatives of the committee argued that the MSV routinely censured advertising, and that on this occasion, by referring the matter to an independent arbiter, the Royal College of Physicians, it was distancing itself from any possible complaint of personal prejudice. If the Royal College upheld the allegation of impropriety, the MSV would be vindicated, but if it rejected the allegation, the concerns of the MSV would be viewed as folly. Yet, not to have acted, or to have deferred action, would have been criticised even more than acting.

An avalanche of criticisms of candidates and the committee followed over the next few days, together with numerous letters to the newspapers, as well as considerable satirical comments, cartoons and doggerel. One commentator criticised the University of Melbourne for appointing Springy to a senior lectureship when he was but a junior in the profession, though hoping that he would 'get on' in due course. This drew a sharp, though anonymous, response in the letters:

> Surely the University knows its own business best, and is well able to look after its own interests. Never in any other University have I heard of senior men for senior posts, and junior men for junior posts. Age does not mean ability. Universities elect lecturers for known ability, and take small account of a man's years. I have no doubt that Dr Springthorpe's successes make many envious, and gain him many detractors. One good trait in the Russell street practitioner is his wish that Dr Springthorpe 'may get on.' Amongst other things, he told your reporter that; but I infer, from the other things that Dr Springthorpe's getting on is somewhat too fast just now to be pleasing. The getting on after the manner of a snail would apparently better please the Russell street doctor. Human nature prompts me to take the side of the weak against the strong; the side of the oppressed against the oppressor; the side of the one against the many. Might, as exemplified by the Medical Society, is not necessarily right. If the majority of hospital subscribers are of my way of thinking, they can show their practical sympathy for Dr Springthorpe on 18th inst. Not being a Melbourne Hospital candidate, publicity therefore not being a necessity for me, I shall adopt a nom de plume. I enclose my card and am—Yours, &c. MEDICO.[28]

At the special meeting, Springy put forward his view that his circular did not significantly differ from the cards of other candidates, and that others had also issued circulars, but had not received the same censure.

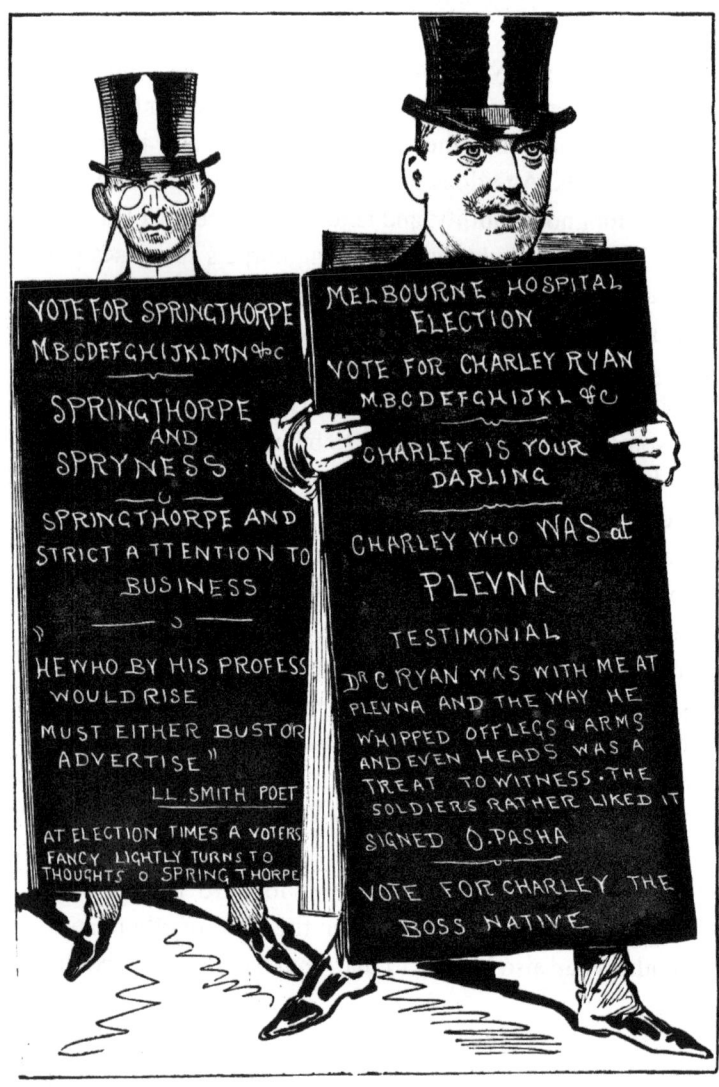

Figure 9: 'What steam is to machinery...'

A Formidable Man

MELBOURNE PUNCH.

A QUESTION OF MEDICAL ETIQUETTE.

1. He was a duly qualified medical man, M.B., O.K., L.C.P., and all that. But one day he forgot himself and said to a patient, "How are YOU to-day?" instead of "how are WE to-day?"

3. And the President instantly summoned a meeting of the society, and they all came and brought their most deadly instruments of torture with them.

2. When it came to the ears of the President of the Medical Society, it took him so badly that you might have knocked him down with a speculum.

4. And they decided to blister him and then saw him into pieces. But he didn't see it and simply putting his finger to their diagnose he went on his way rejoicing.

Figure 10: 'A question of medical etiquette'

There was a heated discussion, with many speaking strongly against Springy's circular as unseemly advertising, and others speaking just as strongly against the way the matter had been handled. A motion was proposed, 'that the committee of the Medical Society acted in an arbitrary way in singling out Dr Springthorpe's circular for action thereon, without reference to the general body of the Society first'. But an amended motion was then proposed, 'that the Medical Society of Victoria endorse the action of the committee in respect of the circular issued by Dr Springthorpe to the governors and subscribers of the Melbourne Hospital'. The amended motion was carried by fifty votes to fourteen.[29]

Election day arrived (18 August 1887), and extraordinary scenes were witnessed, unlike at any election before it. *The Argus* reported at length the following day on the unusually large turnout; 'a strong stream of voters' poured into the Melbourne Athenaeum from 9 a.m. until 4 p.m., with police required to keep people in order:

> The stream, in its course, had to encounter obstacles in the form of canvassers. At no previous election of this kind have touters for votes been so numerous and energetic as they were yesterday. Amongst them were men of all classes— merchants and bookmakers, medical students and grey-headed citizens of renown, doctors and paid canvassers.
>
> The bookmakers mustered strongly, apparently to promote the interests of two of the candidates. Noisiest and most energetic among the canvassers, however, were a number of the medical students, who had a thoroughly good time of it, enjoying themselves immensely. They chiefly supported Dr. Williams and Mr. Girdlestone. Altogether there must have been about 200 canvassers, through whom the voters had to run the gauntlet before they could enter the hall. The canvassers swarmed first up to the door of the polling-room and electors experienced some difficulty in getting into the room, but the police were called in, and kept the canvassers off the stairs in the hall.
>
> For a time, too, the police endeavoured to keep the crowd outside the building from blocking the footpath, but they had to give up the attempt in despair. Several of the candidates

themselves were present during the whole or greater part of the day, 'catching the eyes' of voters and chatting with their friends and supporters. Dr. Springthorpe, the candidate whose circular to the electors created such a ferment in the profession, was not noticed at the scene of the contest yesterday. Some of the electors came from distant parts of the colony to record their votes, and an excited crowd remained outside the Athenaeum waiting for the result of the poll until it was posted up, shortly after 10 o'clock, in the window of Mr. Gould, chemist, Collins street east.[30]

Four physicians and four surgeons to inpatients, and five surgeons to outpatients, had to be elected. Of the nine candidates for the posts of physicians to inpatients, Springy came in third, and was thus elected. To rub salt in the MSV's wound, the reply to its letter to the Royal College of Physicians, received a couple of months later, read in part:

As your communication does not state that the issue of that circular is an infringement of any local law or regulation, and as it does not differ from circulars issued by fellows and members of this college under like circumstances, I shall feel obliged by your stating for the information of the council of this college why the Medical Society of Victoria has addressed the council on this matter.[31]

A leader attributed to the *Daily Telegraph* added more salt:

The purists of the Medical Society of Victoria must be very sorry that they ever raised the question of professional etiquette over the celebrated circular of Dr. Springthorpe. They had the paradoxical satisfaction of knowing that they contributed very largely to the election of the gentleman whose position they were trying to prejudice; and now they have received a crushing blow from the infallible authority to whose decision they so confidently appealed …

We were told that Dr. Springthorpe had committed some dreadfully unprofessional act by letting his qualifications be known by means of a circular to the subscribers, and a whole number of doctors, who had not been guiltless of issuing circulars themselves very little different in character, lifted up their eyes in holy horror. The audacious offender must be brought to book, and so his heinous conduct was referred to the college of physicians from which he obtained his diploma. We do not know exactly what punishment was expected to fall upon his devoted head; but certainly, from the importance attached to the imputed offence, some very terrible penalty was expected. And now comes this letter, politely, but with crushing sarcasm, asking, for the information of the Royal College of Physicians, why the Medical Society of Victoria has addressed the council on the matter. The circular, says this undoubted authority, does not differ from circulars issued by fellows and members of this college under existing circumstances. So there has been no breach of professional etiquette after all, the purists have shown nothing but their ignorance, and all this fuss and irritation of feeling had no better foundation than the busybodyism of a few individuals. Dr Springthorpe has won all round, so he can afford to be generous. The drafting of the letter of reply to the Royal College of Physicians will be quite sufficient punishment for Professor Allen.[32]

Melbourne *Punch* also had its say, by means of a satirical cartoon titled 'Scene in the hall of medical infallibility':

Figure 11: 'Scene in the hall of medical infallibility'

Springy had arrived. Resolving to devote his time primarily to the Melbourne Hospital, he resigned as honorary pathologist to the Alfred Hospital, where he was replaced by Dr Henry Maudsley. But his enemies on the committee of the MSV, not to be deterred, made a further complaint to the Royal College of Physicians at the next election of Melbourne Hospital medical staff four years later. This time, however, they engineered the complaint to be sent by the Medical Board of Victoria, an official government agency. Again, the Royal College pointed out that the information did not differ in any respect from that customarily issued by candidates and was not considered unethical, and queried why the complaint had been made. The matter was finally laid to rest.

2. A Prospering Career

The Springthorpes' second child, Enid May, was born on 16 January 1889. Mother and child both thrived, much to everyone's relief, given their apprehension after the death of baby Dorothy a little over a year earlier. Springy plunged himself into his work.

Throughout his career, Springy manifested a spirit of enquiry and active involvement. He volunteered for the organising committee of the Intercolonial Medical Congress to be held in Melbourne in January 1889, being a member of the congress's executive committee and secretary of the Section of Hygiene, Forensic and State Medicine, as well as presenting several papers in the Section of Medicine.

He had attended the inaugural congress in Adelaide in August 1887, where he had presented a paper but not been an office-bearer. The paper had been on the administration of anaesthetics. Springy quoted the description of chloroform anaesthesia's stages of induction from Lauder Brunton's *Pharmacology, Therapeutics and Materia Medica*, but offered differing views on the desirable depth of unconsciousness for various operations. He advocated lighter levels of anaesthesia so that some reflex responses, such as coughing and swallowing, would be retained. For example, teeth extraction with some retained reflexes did not impede the operation but resulted in quicker recovery and less risk of cardiac complications. Adenoidectomy with some retained reflexes avoided inhalation of blood.[1]

His first paper at the Melbourne congress was titled 'The hepatic element of disease'. Throughout his writings, Springthorpe placed great emphasis on the effects of body type, particularly on how it could predispose individuals to certain vulnerabilities, and how environmental factors could act on those vulnerabilities. He also sought to identify factors that reduced or worsened such effects. These considerations would then guide his advice on prevention or treatment. In this paper, he put forward his belief that patients with a hepatic body type (approximating to today's endomorphic or heavily built body type) digested protein-rich foods in a way that produced gut toxins, making them more vulnerable to certain illnesses such as rheumatic fever. Not only was this vulnerability made worse by a diet high in proteinoids and the adverse effect of alcohol on the liver, but those factors also worsened the features of the hepatic body type itself. He considered the prevalence of this to be increasing in society and becoming a self-perpetuating problem. His concluding remarks were: 'The cause of this predominance of the hepatic factor amongst us seems threefold: a) extreme variability of our climate / b) amount and nature of alcoholic stimulants / c) excessive use of meat as an article of diet.'[2]

Although medical emphasis today would be on obesity rather than the endomorphic body type, Springthorpe's biopsychosocial approach is commendable. His prescription of weight control, less meat, less alcohol, more vegetables (and more exercise, as advocated in other papers) is certainly in keeping with medical views today. The current surge of interest in the enterobiome also suggests that Springy's thinking may have been well ahead of its time, despite its lack of scientific substantiation.[3]

Springy's second paper was 'The nervous substratum of influenza.'[4] In this, he elaborated on a paper he had written (and published in the *Australian Medical Journal* of October 1885) following the 'Fog fever' influenza epidemic between May and August 1885.[5] It was a further extension of his concept of environmental factors, in this case the influenza germ, affecting individuals differently depending upon vulnerabilities predisposed by different bodily characteristics. In this paper, he speculated that central nervous system pathways out to the body may also deliver vulnerabilities, separately from vulnerabilities caused by body type. He described three symptom clusters that he felt were mediated through cervical sympathetic, glossopharyngeal, or vagal nerve functional fields (nerves that arise in the brain and emerge through the skull, as opposed to common nerve pathways that arise from the spinal cord). Beyond presupposing different individual vulnerabilities, he put no hypothesis to account for why the virus might affect people in these differing patterns.[6]

The third paper that Springy presented in the Medical Section was on a series of cases illustrating localisation in nervous diseases.

Twenty-three cases of neurological disorders were tabulated, showing how clinical signs and symptoms identified where neural pathways were disrupted. The information was set out in a large table, and gave an uncontroversial, orthodox snapshot of a typical neurological caseload.[7]

A final component in the Medical Section was a symposium on typhoid fever. Presented as one of a number of contributions, Springy's paper described his experience of eighty-four cases at the Melbourne Hospital: the average duration of hospitalisation was twenty-six days, eleven patients relapsed, and thirteen died. He also discussed the alternative diagnosis of a gastrointestinal form of influenza.[8]

The congress's Section of Hygiene, Forensic and State Medicine followed the Section of Medicine. The presidential address by Dr Henry N. MacLaurin outlined the mortality rates of diseases in the colonies of Australia and New Zealand.[9] Other contributors then spoke about health matters in their regions, including Springy's on the 'hygienic conditions in Victoria'.[10] He discussed public health under three headings: personal health, public health provisions, and legal regulation.

On the personal level, he felt that the population had ample opportunity for good health, but excessive consumption of meat led to a 'hepatic tendency' (being overweight), which increased people's vulnerability to disease. Alcohol consumption was improving, as was exercise, although holiday-taking was insufficient, and there was a dearth of public baths for the poor. He advocated improved diet and personal hygiene – but, more importantly, government action on inadequate drainage and sewerage, and polluted water supply.

He was critical of town cleaning, open drains and polluted rivers. There was poor drainage of stormwater, building regulations were inadequate, and the methods of removal and disposal of nightsoil were unhygienic. The city water supply was mostly satisfactory, although twenty-five out of one hundred and eighty-five regional supplies were polluted. He blamed contaminated creeks for the high prevalence of rheumatism, diphtheria, typhoid and other diarrhoeal diseases, as well as tuberculosis and hydatid disease.

Springy's role as honorary secretary of the Victorian Branch of the British Medical Society gave added weight to his advocacy, alongside other public health advocates', for improvements to the growing city's sewerage system. From 1893, large-scale works were undertaken in Victoria, with home connections beginning about five years later, leading to a marked reduction in typhoid mortality throughout the colony. The annual mortality rate fluctuated with weather conditions. From a high point of 8.5 deaths per 10,000 of the population in 1890, the annual death rate averaged 3.8 per 10,000 over the decade. In 1900, as the new sewerage system came into action, the rate suddenly dropped to 1.9, and a year later to 1.4 – and has generally remained lower since then. The rates were similar throughout the colony, although very slightly higher in the city.[11]

Springy was of the view that most health-related legislation in Victoria was adequate: the Quarantine Act was working well, as were the Public Health Act, Vaccination Act and Pharmacy Act, although the Medical Practitioners' Act needed amendment to protect against unqualified practitioners.[12]

At the end of the congress, it was resolved that the next would be held in Sydney in 1892. An afternoon garden party was held at the Rupertswood mansion in Sunbury, hosted by Sir William and Lady Clarke. Guests went by train, returning to the city by 6 p.m. As an excursion, on Monday 14 January, some six hundred guests went by train to Port Melbourne, where they embarked on the SS *Courier*. After sailing to Port Phillip Heads, they watched torpedo and artillery practice from the forts before transferring to HMVS *Nelson* for afternoon drinks. Upon return to Melbourne, there was an evening concert at the Athenaeum Theatre.

On 7 November 1890, the Springthorpes' third child, Lancelot John, was born. Both parents were delighted to now have a son as well as a daughter. Springy's medical practice was thriving, and life at Camelot seemed ideal. The professional space downstairs was suitably separated from the home space upstairs.

Figure 12: Camelot, Collins Street, Melbourne

Figure 13a&b: The family at home

At this time, both in his private practice and in his Melbourne Hospital work, a central preoccupation of Springy's was tuberculosis. He pointed out that it was a major problem, which 'accounted for about a quarter of child deaths, a half of young adult deaths, about 16% of the total population mortality'.[13] Many promising young lives were cut tragically short. Sanatoria sprang up to treat 'consumption', on the theory that fresh air and good food could reverse the respiratory symptoms and loss of weight that characterised the commonest form of the illness. The sanatoria established for the wealthy took on the appearance of holiday resorts in the mountains, with social calendars to match, while the poor were provided with rather more austere care at the Melbourne Benevolent Asylum in North Melbourne.

Doctors, of course, were faced with the problems of diagnosis and treatment. Early in Springy's career, there was uncertainty about the cause of tuberculosis. While many believed that it was an acquired disease, there was also a substantial body of opinion that it was a constitutional defect. This had significant ramifications for treatment. There was a certain nihilism that nature had to take its course and that, in keeping with Darwinian theory, the deaths of the constitutionally weaker would leave the rest of the population healthier.

In 1882, the German physician and microbiologist Robert Koch had shown that, in locations of tuberculous infection, such as sputum in lung disease or the weeping from scrofulous sores, there were many rod-shaped micro-organisms with specific staining characteristics for examination under the microscope. These micro-organisms could be cultured in guinea pigs and, when passed to healthy animals, would produce tuberculous infection. The presence of the micro-organisms was both necessary and sufficient to explain tuberculous infection. Koch's 'postulates', his methodology of demonstrating the transmissibility of the disease, became the gold standard of proof of infectiousness.

Although there was no known cure, work began on preparing a vaccine to protect against this feared disease. When Koch reported that he had identified a cure, there was worldwide excitement. He announced that he would demonstrate his proof at a scientific meeting in Vienna in 1891. Springy immediately booked his passage to Europe, hoping to attend the demonstration. However, when he arrived, there was no more space available, and he was forced to wait outside. He tried to bribe his way in, but was unsuccessful. After the event, he did manage to meet Dr Koch, and came away thoroughly convinced that a cure was possible.

Koch presented a material called 'lymph' or 'tuberculin', which, when injected into a person who had been exposed to tubercle bacilli, produced a marked inflammatory reaction, whereas no reaction occurred in persons who had not been exposed. This was therefore a valuable test of tuberculous exposure. It did not necessarily mean that the patient had tuberculosis, because it soon became apparent that many people had overcome their exposure to the bacilli and developed resistance. However, patients with tuberculosis reacted and those who had not been exposed did not, so it was an important advance in diagnostics.

Koch, however, went much further. He believed that the 'lymph' was not merely a consequence of tuberculous infection but was active in conferring resistance. Inspired by the knowledge that Jenner's cowpox protected humans from the ravages of smallpox, he reasoned that lymph would protect against tuberculosis, and even cure it. The medical world was overjoyed. Physicians everywhere sought supplies of the magic lymph to cure their patients; Springy was successful in obtaining some to bring back to Melbourne in 1891. There were some positive reports, but disillusionment soon set in. Seriously ill patients did not respond to the lymph, and, after many reports of failure, the treatment was largely abandoned.

In 1891, yet another of Springy's ill-fated siblings died young. News reached him that his younger brother, Albert, had died at Lee, in Kent, on 15 August, aged just twenty-eight.

The following year, Springy was elected president of the Victorian Branch of the British Medical Society, after having served as honorary secretary for some years. It was also around this time that Springy gained significant notoriety from his involvement in a highly publicised murder in Melbourne, known as the Deeming case. In March 1892, the body of Emily Lydia Mather was discovered buried under the hearthstone of a cottage in the inner suburb of Windsor. The autopsy showed that her head had been badly beaten and her throat cut. Enquiry soon produced a strong case against the prime suspect, one Frederick Bailey Deeming, who (it was later discovered) repeatedly fabricated elaborate stories to ingratiate himself with women victims, and who had courted, married and murdered several under various pseudonyms, until he was finally captured and brought to Emily Mather's coronial inquest. It was found that Deeming had married Mather under false pretences in England in September 1891, and the couple had emigrated to Melbourne, arriving on 15 December. Not two weeks later, Emily was dead. After the discovery of her body and the arrest of Deeming in Western Australia, English authorities dug up the floor of Deeming's house in Lancashire, revealing the bodies of a previous wife and their four children.

In Melbourne, the acting coroner, Springy's friend Dr J. E. Neild, presided under considerable difficulties because of the huge public and press interest in the proceedings. Deeming was represented by Alfred Deakin, who sought a verdict of insanity. Today, such a defence would have a fair chance of success, but in the reigning atmosphere of the time, there was no chance of a Melbourne jury sending Deeming anywhere but to the gallows. Two doctors, J. W. Y. Fishbourne and Springthorpe, gave evidence on Deeming's behalf, supporting the insanity claim, for which they were roundly abused in a leader headed 'The case of the murderer Deeming' in the *Australasian Medical Gazette*. The author had no doubts about Deeming's sanity:

> The deliberate premeditation of the crime as shown by the purchase of cement with the necessary tools for its use, the method with which the murder was committed and the body concealed, show without a shadow of doubt that Deeming was fully aware that the crime he intended committing is forbidden by the laws of God and man, and of the penalty he incurred if detected.[14]

Neild committed Deeming for trial, which was held later that month. He was found guilty and, after an appeal was speedily dismissed, was hanged in May 1892. Springy and Fishbourne had been required to give evidence at short notice without having completed their assessment, and felt that the legal proceedings were being rushed, without giving due weight to other aspects beyond Deeming's culpability. They reported his history of family mental illness, serious childhood disturbance, confinement to an asylum, and numerous major epileptic seizures. They also mentioned the seton scar on his neck and the numerous syphilitic scars on his limbs and trunk, and described his psychological state, which was characterised by exaggerations, distortions, lies, delusions and possible hallucinations. They had recommended Deeming be sent to a mental asylum, where he could be adequately assessed, allowing them time to obtain corroborative evidence from England. However, these requests had been denied. They were also upset that after the execution, the government refused permission for a post-mortem examination.[15]

Springy and his friend William Mullen wrote a paper protesting the unsuitability of the M'Naghten Rules as criteria for judging criminal responsibility of the mentally ill. Mullen had been a forensic medical officer with Springy and a superintendent of Yarra Bend Asylum before graduating in law and becoming a barrister. The paper was presented in September 1892 at the Intercolonial Medical Congress,[16] and followed up in a series of letters to *The Age* newspaper.[17]

The M'Naghten rules had been promulgated in the 1840s by the House of Lords, in the case of a killing by a man with delusions of persecution. They ask the questions: 'Did the accused understand what he was doing?' and 'Did he know that it was wrong?' If the answer to either or both questions is 'No', the accused should be judged not responsible. Springy and Mullen contended that the test was 'wrong in theory, false in fact, cruel in its metaphysical conception, and unreliable in its practical application'.[18]

Although judges and others had complained of its difficulties, the Chief Justice of Victoria ruled that, until a greater degree of unanimity was attained by medical and legal authorities, which would enable parliament or courts of justice to lay down a more exact test of insanity, the M'Naghten test would continue. Springy contended that the time had now arrived for change:

> There is no single test of insanity; there can be no single test for the irresponsibility of the insane. Some insane are responsible for certain, if not all, of their criminal acts; others are completely irresponsible, and there are gradations of responsibility varying with the nature of the act and the state of the insane person. Every case must be considered by its own facts.
>
> Instead of regarding insanity as a matter of conduct, the only practical way of dealing with it, in our opinion, is to look upon

it as a disease of the brain; and defining it for legal purposes as 'a disease of the brain, affecting the intellect, the emotions, and the will, not immediately induced by the default of the individual.' There would then be two questions of fact for the jury to determine:— 1) Has the accused such a disease? 2) Is the crime the outcome of that disease? By such procedure all material evidence might be considered by the jury, the law would lose nothing which it should conserve, and at the same time it would come into harmony with legal advance in other countries, and with medical science throughout the world. The two questions suggested are in themselves simple, and such as any jury can readily understand and apply. Any difficulties that may arise will be due to the intricacies of the particular case. Not only are the questions simple, but they are essentially the questions which should be determined in relation to the alleged crime.[19]

As president of the Victorian Branch of the British Medical Association, Springy was appointed as one of the vice-presidents of the Intercolonial Medical Congress to be held in Sydney in September 1892. He and his colleague William Mullen presented their abovementioned paper. It is interesting that, having argued so cogently for recognition of the degrees of mental illness and criminal responsibility, they did not go the extra step and condemn the dichotomy of guilty/not guilty by reason of insanity, even though a gradation of judicial responses would seem the logical extension of their paper.

At the Sydney congress, Springy also presented a paper on his experience with tuberculin. He put forward the view that it should be used in conjunction with other treatments as part of holistic patient care. To answer specific criticism that tuberculin did not kill the bacterium, he offered an analogy of crop, seed and soil: consumption is the crop, the bacterium is the seed, and the human constitution is the soil. Use of tuberculin was aimed at changing the patient's constitutional resistance to the organism. To kill the organism without strengthening resistance might leave the person vulnerable to further infection.[20]

Notwithstanding general scepticism in the profession, Springy continued to use tuberculin in his practice. He reasoned that it seemed to be a potent medication whose limits had not been sufficiently explored, and that more data was necessary before a final conclusion could be drawn. He acknowledged that it might be too late to be useful for some cases, but for others, it might be possible to build up to high levels of the resistance-inducing lymph while avoiding the adverse inflammatory reactions by gradually increasing the dose. This could be valuable in chronic infections.

This theme of disease as not only the product of a pathogenic agent but also dependent upon the patient's inherited constitutional characteristics and socially mediated body habits was consistent throughout Springy's writings. It was expressed forcefully in his discourse on tuberculosis, but also present in papers on rheumatism, typhoid and other diseases. Into this unifying concept he incorporated other themes, such as eugenics.

At the meeting of the Australian Association for the Advancement of Science held in Brisbane in January 1895, Springy was president of the Hygiene Section. His presidential address gave him the opportunity to expand on this theme: 'Health must be in the first place very largely a matter of inheritance. It is worse than useless—it becomes contrary to natural law—to expect healthy offspring and yet disregard heredity.' After some discussion of inherited constitutional factors, he remarked:

> But enough has been said to indicate how an incalculable amount of disease would be averted, and a corresponding amount of health secured, if only inheritance could be scientifically regulated. How far we are from such attempt must be patent to all. Here, at the end of the nineteenth century, we still take less pains to breed men than to breed any other domestic animal. What we require is not the poor thing called State Legislation, but the wider diffusion of knowledge, and the direction of 'marriage by natural selection' into more satisfactory channels, by closer attention to those underlying factors—opportunity and propinquity.[21]

Springy had been replaced as president of the Victorian Branch of the British Medical Association in 1894 by his long-time friend Felix Meyer. This maintained the schism between the younger members of the profession and 'the old guard' in Victoria that had begun with

James Edward Neild's defection and founding of the branch.[22] A third organisation, the Melbourne Medical Association, had formed in 1891 to unite doctors who had received their training at the University of Melbourne. It now took on a role as mediator between the Medical Society of Victoria and the BMA Victorian Branch, bringing them together on matters of mutual interest such as legislation, hospital appointments and fees. In this capacity, it sponsored the establishment of the Medical Defence Association. However, despite such collaboration and continued lobbying for amalgamation of the MSV and BMA, Neild's opposition successfully prevented this unification until his death in 1906.[23] The two organisations then reconciled and affiliated, providing a foundation for the subsequent formation of the Australian Medical Association.

The fourth Intercolonial Medical Congress was held in Dunedin in 1896, and Springy attended as an official representative of the Victorian Government. Though not a major office-bearer, he chaired the Section of Public Health, and was, as usual, an active member-participant, which included being an invited contributor to the seminar on tuberculosis. In the opening plenary session, when the president raised the topic of including a dental section in the congress, the transactions reported:

> DR SPRINGTHORPE (Melbourne), as a member of the Dental Board of Victoria, remarked that it was partly with the idea of raising the status of dentistry that the proposal for the addition of a dental section was made. Nothing could, however, be done now, and perhaps the best thing would be to instruct the next Congress to take some action in the matter. He moved—'That the question of the establishment of a dental section be transmitted to the Executive Committee of the next Congress with power to take action in the matter.' DR. KNAGGS (Sydney) seconded the motion.
>
> DR. O'HARA (Melbourne) thought it would be an advantage not only to dentists in raising the standard, but also to the profession generally if dentists were admitted to the Congress as a section. He thought, however, that dentists should be brought to a certain standard before being admitted.
>
> The motion was carried without dissent.[24]

At the same session, it was reported that the president laid on the table a memorial from the Women's Christian Temperance Union of Victoria on the subject of the Contagious Diseases Act:

> Dr Springthorpe (Melbourne) moved: "That the memorial be referred to the Public Health Section." As president of that section he was prepared to undertake that it should be brought before the members. Dr Murray-Ainsley (Christchurch) seconded Dr. Springthorpe's motion, and said that other communications might be received from Christchurch.[25]

On the third day of the congress, a seminar was held on 'Tuberculosis in man and animals', with Dr Batchelor (president of the congress) in the chair. Professor Watson of Adelaide opened the seminar, and Springy was invited to deal with 'the medical aspect'.[26] His presentation began with a characterisation of tuberculosis as the single greatest cause of death in Australia at that time, and a description of the infectious nature of the tubercle bacillus. He argued that its wide-ranging manifestations were due to constitutional factors in individuals, and spoke of the complexity added when patients contracted other diseases alongside tuberculosis.

Springy advocated the injection of tuberculin as a diagnostic aid: a local skin reaction would indicate previous exposure to the bacillus, but a feverish reaction would indicate current infection. A series of injections might promote resistance. He asked, rhetorically: 'Will those who decry tuberculin say they have given the remedy this trial?'[27] But in the same paper, he conceded that this treatment was of limited value in fulminant (aggressive) infections.

As well as advocating treatment by lymph injections, Springy was a fervent advocate for stringent public health measures. He supported revising the Public Health laws so that every case of tuberculosis, as an infectious disease, should be legally required to be reported to the Health Department. He also promoted public education on general cleanliness, sterilisation of potentially infected materials, and avoidance of cross-infection from patients with tuberculosis. He also strongly advocated for bacteriological testing for the bacillus. Acknowledging that treatments were very limited, his emphasis turned to prevention:

It will be at once apparent that I place preventive treatment as incomparably before everything else. This requires, of course, to be dealt with both from the bacillary and constitutional points of view. The former includes destruction of all approachable bacilli before their contamination of the environment, the disinfection of infected environment, and the prevention of tubercular infection through air, food and milk. Some, at least, of these requirements demand State interference if they are to be satisfactorily performed; but it lies, in my opinion, at the door of our profession to do infinitely more than is at present attempted. It is almost incredible—yet some years' continued enquiry have conclusively proved to me—that scarcely a percentage of medical men give any instructions worthy [of] the name for the destruction or disinfection of the sputum, and less still, make any enquiry into the condition of the dairy from which the milk of their sick children is obtained, or direct that the unknown milk should be scalded before use.[28]

In addition to patient-centred hygiene, Springy supported the campaign against spittoons and spitting. Because of this, a number of public places (such as the city of Melbourne's main railway station, Flinders Street, which was built at the turn of the 20th century) still have glazed tiles on the walls instructing 'DO NOT SPIT'. He also advocated pasteurisation of milk, and veterinary inspection of dairy and abattoir facilities to combat spread of bovine tuberculosis. In a letter to *The Brisbane Courier*, Springy urged the employment of public health meat inspectors, by quoting from the medical journal *The Lancet*:

Certainly the most remarkable feature about the Berlin slaughterhouse is the extensive precaution taken to prevent the sale of diseased meat. There is an enormous pavilion, which contains six divisions, in each of which 36 persons are employed, half male, half female, and all constantly employed in the microscopic examination of samples, for the most part of pork.' [sic] Who, and how many, are our inspectors?[29]

In the same letter, he advocated the testing of live cattle for tuberculosis:

> As regards the commercial aspect, take the action of the Danish government, one of our main rivals in the butter trade. They are spending £15,000 during the next few years in examining all cattle with the tuberculin test for tubercular disease and destroying all diseased animals so as to have pure herds and pure butter. If worth their while, may it not be worth ours? ... I find that the city of Boston is using the same test, and finding 12% of cattle diseased, and that the Canadian Government have ordered the quarantining of all imported cattle and similar testing. I also understand that Imperial officers are there appointed at the local expense to prevent the shipping of diseased meat into England. Have these facts no importance, present and future, to Queensland stockowners? I think that they have, and on the ground that prevention is better than cure, certainly recommend the prompt consideration of this vital question to all concerned; for our turn may come next, and there are already indications that that time is not far distant.[30]

Springy's influence in the public debate was very powerful. He had submitted a long report to the Victorian Government, which was widely quoted in the press. The Victorian Chief Health Officer, Dr Dan Gresswell, when about to speak on bovine tuberculosis at a public meeting in Ballarat a couple of months after the Dunedin conference, was introduced by the following comments on Springthorpe's words:

> I shall read a few extracts from an address by Dr Springthorpe, of Melbourne, taken from 'The Australian Farm and Home', of March 1895, and read at the annual opening of the Melbourne Veterinary College, which, if the Government would have reprinted, and have copies sent to every council in the colony, I am sure, would be productive of much good, and would open the eyes of councillors to the importance of the subject. I seriously commend this to the attention of the Government for the people's health['s] sake.[31]

Springy used every opportunity to advance his ideas. To counter resistance to pasteurisation, he participated in a committee of the Royal Agricultural Society of Victoria, which brought out a report widely covered in the newspapers. Objectors believed, without evidence, that fresh milk had superior taste, nutritional qualities and health benefits. The main conclusion of the report was:

> The Committee, after careful investigation, is satisfied that without any additional cost to the consumer pure milk can be supplied to the inhabitants of Melbourne and suburbs, which will keep sound for 48 hours, and wherein all active germs have been destroyed without the aid of antiseptics. This milk will be perfectly wholesome, and free from the objections brought against milk as ordinarily supplied and treated.[32]

Since Springy's time, the introduction of the BCG (Bacillus Calmette–Guérin) vaccination, public X-ray screening for early detection, and effective antibiotic treatments have greatly reduced the prevalence of tuberculosis in Australia, although it remains a serious global health problem. Its prevalence had actually begun to decline in Europe in the second half of the nineteenth century, even before the public health measures advocated by Springy had been implemented. This observation, and the realisation that sanatoria had not been particularly effective in treatment, led some critics to proclaim that the real reason for the reduction in prevalence was not public health measures, but the improving standard of living: less crowded accommodation, and better ventilation, cleanliness, nutrition and general health.

Notwithstanding that such conditions were in effect what the sanatoria were trying to achieve for their patients, the polarisation of views continued for some years, before the Australian scientist Macfarlane Burnet provided a synthesis of concepts. Burnet said that the natural history of tuberculosis is that a high percentage of people will be exposed to the bacilli, but that the biological defences of the body enable the majority to resist the disease and develop immunity. A proportion will succumb to the disease. Environmental circumstances, the extent of the exposure, and the integrity of the immune system, influenced as it is by general health and wellbeing, will determine whether or not the bacilli take hold. This was substantially what Springy was advocating. In truth, most of the disparate theorists did have some valid comments to make in describing this elephant in the room.

Another paper in the Dunedin congress was presented by Dr W. A. Chapple of Wellington on the public health aspects of alcohol. He described its physiological effects and adverse health consequences, and concluded by advocating public education: 'If these are the true facts about alcohol taken as a beverage in health, we are, as medical men, individually and collectively, in duty and honour bound to make it known to the public, over whose health we pretend to preside.'[33] But the subsequent discussion was almost entirely unsupportive. The most typical response was that of Dr Stenhouse, who said that:

> the subject of alcoholism was not one that he had given very much attention to. Dr. Chapple seemed to imagine that his case was true if he could show, on the one hand, that a moderate consumption of alcohol was not necessary to the health of the body, and if he could also show, on the other hand, that the consumption of alcohol in excess was detrimental to the body. But that was not sufficient, because if it could be shown that the moderate consumption of alcohol added somewhat to the pleasures of life, if it diffused happiness among mankind to some extent without being injurious, that was a great matter, seeing that we were not living in an ideal world, and that the world was full of ups and downs, of anxieties and sorrows of one kind or another. He was sure, from his own observation, that the moderate use of alcohol, on times and occasions, was beneficial, and that it enabled many a man to tide over a period of depression.[34]

Springy took the opportunity to close the alcohol discussion with his own biopsychosocial formulation. This was described in the Congress Proceedings, revealing his views of the motivations behind addictive behaviour:

> It was a matter of great complexity, and although they [the congress] all saw the evil effects of excess in the use of alcohol,

he [Springy] did not think Dr. Chapple had gone deep enough down. The fact was that the human race in civilized parts was not absolutely and permanently healthy. Every race on the globe seemed more or less irresistibly drawn to a stimulo-sedative of some sort—if it was not alcohol it was hashish, opium, tea, or some other stimulant. It was not merely a question of craving, it was an absolute instinct. He tried to fancy that the instinct was produced by there not being a proper adjustment between the individual and his environments, and by the use of one of these stimulo-sedatives the individual got a temporary adjustment— he got into a paradise for a time; it was a fool's paradise, of course, but it was the only sort of paradise he could get into. This for a time seemed to make a not perfectly healthy individual comfortable, happy, cosy, and until they gave him a better paradise he would get into this one. They might prohibit his liquor and he would go in for stimulant in some other form. In Ireland they went in for ether drinking, and there were cocaine-ists, morphia-ists, and all sorts of 'ists.' Take a healthy individual and a healthy environment, and then he would not want the stimulant; but until they did this he would continue to want it, and though they might prohibit it he would get it. Drinking was said to be the cause of many things, but he ventured to say it was rather the measure of extent of these things. It was said to be the cause of unhappiness, but he regarded it as the measure of the effort of a man to get into the happiness he had not got. Dr. Chapple's paper was the pathology of alcohol and not the physiology, and what they wanted was the physiology of it. It seemed to him that the prohibitionist did not go deep enough down—he saw the unhappiness and presumed that the cause was this one thing, which was not the only cause. The misuse was due to two things. The first was the temperament of the individual; and in that connection he said people of neuritic temperament ought to be warned against the dangers of alcohol. The second thing was the unsuitable environment. The over-worked and poor who were not in a happy condition and not likely to get into one— these were the people who took to liquor, and having once taken to it misused it. [35]

Dr Stenhouse also presented a paper on educational

problems affecting health.[36] His main proposition was that schoolwork should not begin before age seven, because earlier schoolwork was rote learning that permanently impaired imagination, reflection and reasoning. For the same reason, he opposed kindergarten before the age of five, and teaching according to curriculum standards, in favour of the child's interests determining what is taught. He did not support giving women the same education as men, 'because they are designed by Nature to fulfil different purposes'.[37]

There was substantial dissent from these views. Springy drew the discussion to a close by saying that the subject was so large that more time might be devoted to it at a future congress. His own view was that 'Nature is always educating, and man simply added. The question was how that addition should take place. He was one of those who thought that a wise kindergarten should be introduced into the public schools in place of the standard teaching for young children.'[38]

The congress's Section of Public Health opened with Springy's presidential address, which he titled 'The battle of life'.[39] This gave him the opportunity to expound on his favourite themes around constitutional factors in health. He began with Darwin's concept of natural selection being a battle of life: 'As in ordinary warfare, other things being equal, the battle is won by the best selected, best trained soldiery, so in the battle of life the issue depends primarily upon heredity and development'. Although not explicitly commenting on eugenics, he did say, 'There is no gift given the young life that can compare with that of healthy parentage. Yet, by thousands of thousands the inherited momentum continues towards weakness.' According to him, other aspects of healthy development, 'the important questions of food, drink, exercise, rest, occupation and the like', together with combatting illnesses, placed the physician in the role of 'helping the fighter fight better'. Nevertheless, he counselled against all-out war on germs, foreshadowing a twenty-first-century enthusiasm for the enterobiome:

> Not unnaturally, perhaps, it has become too much the custom to regard all microbes as injurious, forgetful of the fact that there is another side to these activities, as is exemplified in

their being nature's scavengers and earth's fertilisers, bakers of man's bread, brewers of his beer, makers of his vinegar, and flavourers of his wine, butter and cheese. Indeed, without the presence of friendly germs in his intestinal flora, his food would not be peptonised, and in the midst of plenty he would starve. Another common error is the supposition that the invasion of the germ necessitates the production of the disease. This is no doubt true in certain cases, such as anthrax and certain pyococci, but it is generally the constitutional state rather than the presence of the germ which determines the extent of infection and the issue of the fight.[40]

Springy's attention then turned deftly from the microscopic to the macro, as he discussed public health programs and legislation. He had been deeply impressed by a paper presented at the Indian Medical Congress in January 1895, and proposed it as a model for nationwide health administration across the soon-to-be federated colonies of Australia.

The scheme covered service delivery at local, provincial and statewide levels. The local authority would be responsible for building regulation, water supply and sanitary services and local application of public health regulations. The provincial authority would monitor the effectiveness of local services and provide specialist and research facilities. It would also give advice on desirable changes to the regulatory framework. The statewide level would collate and publish population data, plan future developments and liaise with Government for legislative and financial support to all levels.[41] A motion that this scheme be brought to the attention of colonial governments was proposed and passed.

The *Otago Witness* newspaper reported that in the closing address of the congress, its president (Dr Batchelor) had said:

There was one very bad mistake made in connection with the Congress—he was going to confess it now—and that was that they did not take the biggest hall in town and invited [sic] every member of the community to come and listen to the address by Dr Springthorpe on public health.— (Applause). It was the most intellectual, brilliant, and heart-inspiring address he (Dr

Batchelor) had ever had the pleasure of listening to. The address was not a technical one and he would advise every person in town to read it. If it was only for that address the congress was worth being held.— (Applause.)[42]

After the congress, Springy wrote a report for the Premier of Victoria, which he had been authorised to do as the government's official representative to the Public Health Section. In it he quoted the resolutions of the congress, emphasising his support for the actions recommended regarding tuberculosis, public sanitation and public health regulations. As his official status had been granted on condition that he paid his own expenses, he was unable to resist a reminder: 'I trust, however, that the present will not be held as establishing a precedent as regards expenses, but that the Victorian Government will place subsequent representatives upon the same financial footing as those of other Australian Governments'.[43]

Annie had accompanied her husband to the Dunedin congress, and two events involving her participation were noted. The first was a garden party hosted by Dr Batchelor at the Dunedin Club. Guests included the Governor of New Zealand, Lord Glasgow, and the premier, Mr Ward, along with their wives. They were entertained by the Naval Artillery Band and the Faust Family of Bell-Ringers.[44] The other was a Saturday trip to Mount Cook, which involved camping out and climbing the Mueller Glacier. The party included twenty-three doctors (all men) and five women, but Annie was the only woman to take part in the more strenuous activity of the glacier climb.[45] She had always enjoyed bushwalking, although her main sporting enthusiasm was cycling. She and Springy frequently went on long bike rides, which were sometimes reported in the newspapers.

Springy was an enthusiastic cyclist, although he still felt that cycling was 'inadvisable in the young, because from their immaturity distortion of spine and disproportionate development of heart and leg were too probable. But for those who had to work indoors it offered advantages that could be found in no other form of exercise.' For adults, he advised: 'Mechanics, machinists, workers in shops and factories—to such the cycle opens up new and healthier exercise. It means more room and less overcrowding, more country and less towns, less smoking and less drinking. It alters environment as nothing else has ever attempted.'[46]

Cycling was still a relatively new sport at this time. Wooden-spoked velocipedes had enjoyed a brief vogue in the 1860s, and by 1870 the more graceful high bicycle, or 'penny farthing', had been developed in England, and was soon imported to Australia. For nearly twenty years, it was the fastest thing on the road. The Melbourne Bicycle Club was formed in 1878, the Sydney Bicycle Club the following year, and other clubs quickly followed. By 1890, the safety bicycle had been developed to a standard design, and quickly replaced the high bicycle. Safety bicycles heralded a new wave of adventure all over the world: by 1894, Americans were crossing Asia on safety bicycles, the type of machine that the Springthorpes rode.[47] The problem of women's long Victorian skirts was solved by the introduction of 'rational dress'. This took several forms: riding skirts divided into two parts like French culottes; knickerbockers (trousers gathered in below the knees and worn with long socks); or bloomers (baggy trousers tied around the ankles).

Figure 14: Cyclist Annie Springthorpe

Of one long ride in the summer of 1895, a newspaper reported: 'Some interest was excited at Lilydale by the arrival of Dr. and Mrs Springthorpe, of Melbourne, on bicycles. They had ridden from the city that afternoon. Mrs Springthorpe wore the rational dress and did not seem at all fatigued after her journey.'[48] The distance from Melbourne to Lilydale is about forty kilometres as the crow flies – a solid ride in one afternoon.

In April 1897, Springy became the inaugural president of the Victorian Amateur Cyclists' Union.[49] This took the place of the Victorian Amateur Cycling Council, which was a subcommittee of the Victorian Amateur Athletic Association. He was re-elected at a general meeting later that year.[50] In 1898, a merger was proposed between the union and the League of Victorian Wheelmen, an alternative organisation that included most of the state's professional cyclists. There was considerable debate about whether a merger would jeopardise the amateur status of non-professional members and damage the character of the sport. Springy felt that the professionals and amateurs could coexist, and that the interests of all would be furthered by a comprehensive body. Although the debate dragged on, the merger was eventually successful, maintaining amateurs' statuses alongside professionals'.

All seemed to be going well when Annie became pregnant with their fourth child, due in March 1897. But in December, she began to experience ante-partum bleeding complications. Specialists decided that there was placenta praevia, and that a caesarean section would be performed on Saturday 23 January 1897. The premature baby boy, Guy Annis Springthorpe, was ill but survived. His mother died of uncontrollable post-partum haemorrhage. Springy was devastated.

Annie was buried on 26 January, which would have been her thirtieth birthday, and the couple's tenth wedding anniversary. The burial was held privately at Booroondara Cemetery in Kew, attended by fifteen mourners. Before closing Annie's coffin lid, Congregational minister Dr Bevan christened little Guy, who had been born just as Annie died. Lancelot (aged six) and Enid (aged eight) were soon sent to live with their maternal grandparents in Gippsland, and baby Guy to his maternal aunt, Florence Inglis, in Kew. Springy began a prolonged period of mourning.

3. Bereavement

'Dead. Dead. What does it mean?'

Springy's grief poured out in his diary – not just immediately, but recursively for more than a decade.1 Eighteen months after Annie's death, he observed: 'The sense of loss has grown, the hunger of the soul continues, there has not been a day in which my lost love has not occupied all my spare time. I love her better even than before.' He could not yet accept the truth, and continued to call her back, beseeching: 'Can't you come back? Have you gone "for all time"? It seems incredible!'[2] And a month later: 'My heart is broken for her. I do nothing, outside my work, but think, think of her.' His grief reflected not only his own religious beliefs but also the Victorian conventions of mourning.[3]

In private, Springy turned the family home into a shrine to Annie. He gathered all her memorabilia into a library 'consecrated to her memory', and decided to:

> make our bedroom redolent of memories of her; its walls and surfaces covered with photographs, cards, paintings etc, fundamentally associated with her married life. For since she cannot be present in the body I must do the next best thing, surround myself with reminders and transform the house of desolation into the haunt of blessed memories I have kept— too soon to fade—the very blood stains on the matting, the loss of which cost her her dear life. Thus, I can shut the door of the bedroom and in fancy go over some of the happy past and in my heart hold communion with my lost love. And the rest of the house will remain so long as possible, just as she left it.[4]

In addition to his commemorative archive, Springy commissioned an elaborate 'In Memoriam' book, which, after Camelot, was the second step in his memorialisation process.[5] It was designed by distinguished Victorian artist John Longstaff, who had painted Annie's portrait as a young woman and who was subsequently to contribute to the design of her tomb. The book, like Springy's diary, was a private memorial to Annie.

Springy started the book a month after Annie's death, and had it bound in a black morocco cover on which lay a photograph of Annie. He distributed copies only to family and very close friends about five months later. It included poems, photographs, and idealised memories of Annie as 'self- sacrificing, modest, tender and true, grateful, tactful and wise'. Springthorpe visualised this volume as an important method of perpetuating Annie's influence.[6]

A Formidable Man

Farewell, a long farewell to all.

SELF-SACRIFICING, MODEST, TENDER, AND TRUE, GRACEFUL, TACTFUL, AND WISE.

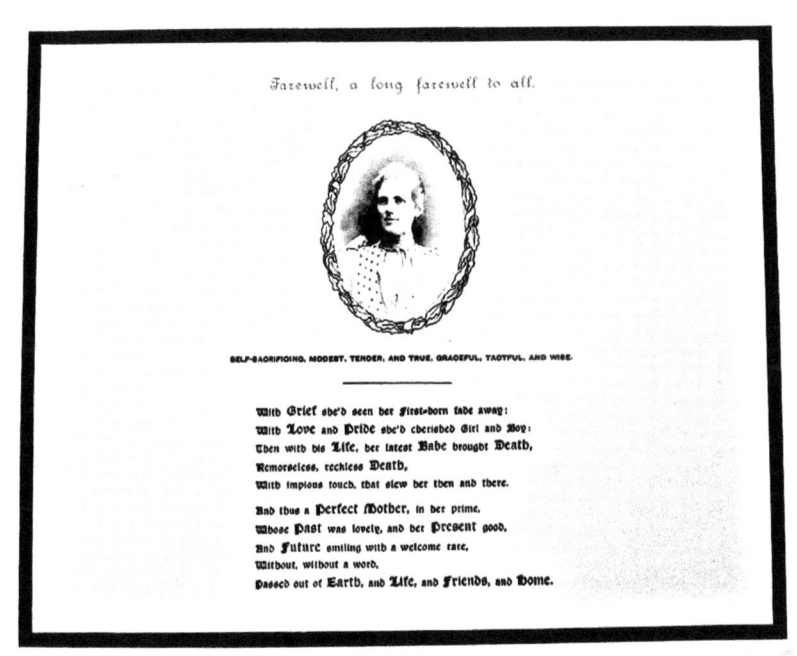

With Grief she'd seen her First-born fade away;
With Love and Pride she'd cherished Girl and Boy;
Then with his Life, her latest Babe brought Death,
Remorseless, reckless Death,
With impious touch, that slew her then and there.

And thus a Perfect Mother, in her prime,
Whose Past was lovely, and her Present good,
And Future smiling with a welcome face,
Without, without a word,
Passed out of Earth, and Life, and Friends, and Home.

In Sad and Sacred memory
of one
Beloved by all who knew her

A pattern daughter, a perfect mother, an ideal wife

Her life a lyric

But her sudden and untimely death

A tragedy

Figure 15: In Memoriam – 1

Figure 16: In Memoriam – 2

The book combined all the joint 'relics' of the married couple which Springthorpe could find for his 'private album'. For the public memorial, Springy called on long-time friends and associates. He decided to build a magnificent tomb, which would be 'a lifelong task in its care and attention, a something that will continue to bind me to Her it commemorates so long as I live'. He asked one of Melbourne's younger but already prominent architects, Harold Desbrowe-Annear, to design the tomb. The idea had come to him while Annie's body lay in state in the drawing room at Camelot, in the days before her funeral. He had thought, 'put this in marble':

> For on the Tuesday after her burial I sent home to [Bertram] Mackennal an appeal for a masterpiece of sculpture—all in white marble, a sarcophagus, richly traced, with certain inscriptions on the sides—on the top, a sculptured figure, as much like Annie as she lay in the drawing room as possible with imitation posies, lilies, etc.—at the foot a beautiful female figure (like Balter's Medea in Jacobs' Wonder Voyages) representing human sorrow and love—at the head, a strong but sympathetic angel, typifying Immortal Love and all under a canopy, primarily protective against wind and weather, but at the same time [a] decorative part of the design like the Alhambra roofing and the perforated carvings of the Taj.[7]

The tomb was to be his symbolic idealised representation: 'the whole is more than a Tomb—it is the Real made Ideal—an apotheosis of love for all true lovers to the end of Time with its tale of loss, memory, separation and Reunion'.[8]

On 14 March 1899, more than two years after Annie's death, Springy wrote to the trustees of the Boroondara Cemetery requesting a site eighty feet (twenty-four metres) square, with a central area of twenty feet (six metres) square for the erection of a temple. In April, he was shown the site, which offered fine views of the surrounding countryside. He commissioned William Guilfoyle, curator of Melbourne's Royal Botanic Gardens, to landscape the grounds of the temple, planting Western Australian flowering red gum trees and planning a 'Garden of the Dead'.

Building the memorial was Springy's major preoccupation for the next year and a half. The design by Desbrowe-Annear features twelve columns of deep-green granite imported from Scotland, supporting a superstructure of white Harcourt granite. The domed glass roof, created by Brooks, Robinson & Co., Melbourne's leading firm of stained-glass artisans at the time, is in tones of deep red, purple and orange arranged in a radiating pattern, and sits in the rectangular form behind the classical pediments;[9] refer to Figure 17 on page 93. The bronze work was by Marriotts of Melbourne. James Marriott was an award-winning metalwork artist and designer, who worked with Desbrowe-Annear on projects such as the decorative arches that adorned Princes Bridge for the royal visit celebrating Federation in 1901.

The memorial incorporates very extensive, complex symbolism. This is well documented in the monograph by Joseph Lis, *The Love That Never Dies: The Secret Symbolism of the Springthorpe Memorial* and further elaborated by Professor Pat Jalland in *Australian Ways of Death* (2002) and 'Magnificent Obsession' (2002). In summary:

> Just about every flat surface of the memorial has something written on it. The inscriptions in English and archaic Greek were composed by Thomas Tucker, professor of classics at the University of Melbourne. Around the pediment are verses from the Bible written in Greek. The floor has a geometric mosaic with four rectangles of glazed red tiles bearing inscriptions of poetic and religious significance. One is the first stanza of *The Blessed Damozel* by Dante Gabriel Rosetti: 'The Blessed Damozel leans out from the gold bar of Heaven; / Her eyes are deeper than the depth of water stilled at even; / She has three lilies in her hand, and the stars in her hair are seven'. The three lilies are a reference to the Holy Trinity, and the seven stars to Jesus in Revelations 1:16: 'In His right hand he held seven stars'. Another inscription is from Dante's *The New Life*, Canto 23, written in 1295, and refers to angels flying to Heaven where 'There shall all things be made clear'.[10] Others are from poems by Robert and Elizabeth Browning, and Alfred, Lord Tennyson.[11] Nowhere does Annie's name appear, only the words:
> My own true love,

Pattern daughter perfect mother and ideal wife,
Born on the 26th day of January 1867
Married on the 26th day of January 1887
Buried on 26th day of January 1897.

On 18 July 1899, in the presence of her husband and three children, Annie's remains were disinterred and relocated to a family vault over which the new monument would be constructed. This was, itself, an emotionally disturbing event, although Springy had resolved to remain unaffected by it. He had insisted that his children be present because, as outlined by Jalland, the tomb would one day hold their bodies, so he believed they ought to be there for its establishment.[12] The remains of little Dorothy Anne, their first child, who had died in 1887, were also moved.[13]

On 2 October 1899, Springy received from Mackennal two photographs of the memorial sculpture that he had created for Annie's grave. Springy noted in his diary:

> A visitor from Heaven just alighted at the Tomb. Divinity shining through her garments. Purity throned in her face. In her hands a crown of lilies.
>
> So ends our quest, proud Mackennal. On a fitting sarcophagus, regal in design, lies the recumbent figure of my Love, with lilies on the breast, at Her feet Human grief bends low, with tear dried eye, and over Her head, a glorious Angel, sent by Divine Love—the Love that never dies.
>
> Thanks, friend—it is a masterpiece.[14]

As the public unveiling of the memorial grew closer, Springthorpe worried whether the perfection of his dream could ever be achieved in reality. But he realised that his fears were unfounded when he finally gazed with wonder at the angels and the recumbent figure of his wife, in the presence of the Mackennals, with whom he had formed a close friendship.[15] Refer to Figure 18 on page 94.

Springy was completely satisfied with the achievement: 'It is simply perfect in Conception, execution, Holiness—all that I could ask or think ... I am entranced by the whole'.[16] Unveiled on 26 January 1901, the fourth anniversary of Annie's death, the memorial rapidly became a major public attraction. Crowds would travel by tram to the cemetery at weekends to view it. Springy's delight with the spectacular memorial was echoed by observers at the time – *The Bulletin* was deeply impressed by 'sculptor Mackennal's transcendent genius' – and has been ever since.[17]

Just over a decade later, Springthorpe decided to extend the memorial. He had the grounds re-landscaped to include a rectangular pool, two seats, a sundial and two newly commissioned sculptures. In this project, he sought the advice of a horticulturalist, Charles Loughman, and employed the young sculptor Charles Web Gilbert to produce two works.

One, titled *Love and Death*, depicts a brolga defending her chicks against a snake rearing up to strike.[18] The other, *The Wheel of Life*, portrays a monk, carved as a relief on a block of marble housed under a bronze pagoda roof, the corners of which originally formed two dragon heads (now lost), while the ridges are the spikes of a dragon's back. [19] This sculpture was said to be based on the Tibetan master in Rudyard Kipling's *Kim*. It was described in 1925 in the following terms:

> The Chinese pilgrim seated at the wayside, his prayer wheel and begging bowl set down beside him, is meditating, thinking at last he has attained peace and security, and all the while the wheel of fate spins over lines guided by a wonderful hand, Chinese, and with long fingernails which somehow suggest the talons of a vulture, or, perhaps, some fabulous vampire monster. Trailing across the lower left-hand corner is the lotus flower with its significance of ease and beauty.[20]

Figure 19: Web Gilbert's 'Wheel of Life'

These sculptures are not at the memorial, and it is unclear whether they were ever placed there. There has been some discussion that the Tibetan sculpture, in particular, was thought 'unsuitable' because it did not fit in with the Christian theme of the tomb. They were later displayed in the garden of Springthorpe's new house, 'Joyous Gard' in Murrumbeena, in an isolated spot of wild native bushland that Springy called his 'forest'.[21] After his death, *The Wheel of Life* was advertised among the contents of Joyous Gard that were auctioned on 15 May 1934.[22] In 1936, it was donated to the Medical School of the University of Melbourne in honour of Dr Lilian Helen Alexander (1861–1934), one of the first two women to study medicine at the university.[23] There it remains, but the whereabouts of the brolga group is unknown.

Sadly, most of the memorial gardens were subsumed by the cemetery after Springthorpe's death, apparently because of a failure to finalise permanent tenure. Nevertheless, the tomb remains a truly remarkable funerary monument, in both Australian and international terms.

4. Life After Annie

Notwithstanding his grief and preoccupation with memorials, Springy continued his medical work unabated after Annie's death. As president of the Melbourne Medical Association, in 1900, he saw an opportunity to use his growing influence. He had been promoting collaboration between the Medical Society of Victoria and the British Medical Association Victorian Branch, despite Neild's opposition to amalgamation. However, the process was significantly complicated by a medico-political incident.

Springy was re-elected to the council of the British Medical Association Victorian Branch in 1899 in the role of 'Editor'. Shortly afterwards, his friend and colleague John Fishbourne complained of what he perceived as unethical behaviour by a Melbourne Hospital surgeon colleague, Henry O'Hara. The complaint was based on a leaflet by the Silenette Company spruiking a device to deposit an intravaginal powder that would act as a contraceptive. The ethical breaches were that doctors were prohibited from using or advocating 'secret remedies', were expected to advocate against such unproven treatments, and were forbidden to have a role or financial interest in companies providing them.

Springy enthusiastically took up the cause. Enquiries to the Registrar-General's Department revealed that O'Hara was listed as a director of the company and the owner of two thousand shares. The council concluded that O'Hara had committed a serious breach of ethics. He was asked to appear before it and show cause why he should not be expelled. In his submission, he claimed that he had no involvement in the company. He said that the negotiations to form it, patent the device and use his name had all been undertaken by acquaintances trying to exploit his standing in the profession for the benefit of their business. The shares had been allocated without his knowledge, and he had never claimed them. He repudiated ownership. Nevertheless, the February 1900 meeting of the council voted to expel him.

The ordinary monthly meeting of the Victorian Branch of the British Medical Association was held in the Medical Society Hall in Albert Street, East Melbourne, on Wednesday 21 March 1900. The president, Mr G. A. Syme, was in the chair, and there were also present Drs Brett, Beattie-Smith, Hamilton Russell, and Maudsley, along with seventy-eight other members.[1] The business of the meeting was to confirm the expulsion of Mr H. M. O'Hara from the branch, as had been resolved by a three-fourths majority of council at its February meeting. The complaint, the evidence and the explanation in defence were presented to the meeting. Mr O'Hara's statement denying involvement in the company was supported by testimony from his solicitor, Mr Montague Cohen, and Silenette's director, Mr F. W. Loxton. During the discussion, Springy highlighted inconsistencies in past and present information provided by Mr Cohen. Some of Mr O'Hara's friends objected that this had not been part of the information leading to the initial decision. Springy was accused of being investigator, prosecutor, judge and jury. There was discussion of why the council had not seen fit to propose a lesser penalty than expulsion, but this was justified on the grounds of consistency standards. The president then put forward the motion to expel O'Hara, which was approved forty-four votes to thirty-four. But as this did not constitute three-fourths of the council, it was declared lost. The whole council then resigned. The meeting was widely reported in the newspapers.[2]

A month later, a new council was elected, with Dr James Neild as president and a predominance of members who had supported Dr O'Hara. The new secretary, Dr W. B. Vance, was critical of Springy's contribution to the case, and there was a short war of words between the lawyer Cohen and Springy about whose contributions were most trustworthy. The new council, however, took a somewhat more conciliatory tone when the New South Wales Branch suggested that the British Medical Society should undertake a full investigation into the circumstances leading to the resignation of the previous Victorian Branch Council. Correspondence on the subject was finally drawn to a close by the editor of the *Australasian Medical Gazette* in its August 1900 edition.[3]

Springy felt that the medical profession should use its position of leadership to encourage other health professions to improve their training, quality of care, and standing in the community. He was especially interested in nursing. Together with his friend Felix Meyer, who became editor of their journal, *UNA*, Springy helped to found the Victorian Trained Nurses Association, becoming its first president in 1901. In the first half of the nineteenth century, nursing had been an untrained occupation, considered largely like housework, but more disreputable. Its importance for patients' recovery was demonstrated by the work of Florence Nightingale during the Crimean War. Her methods of training nurses were widely acknowledged in the 1860s, and six of her trainees were recruited to bring her methods to Australia, arriving in February 1868. Barely two weeks later, on 12 March 1868, there was an attempted assassination of Prince Alfred, the second son of Queen Victoria, in Sydney. Two of the Nightingale-trained nurses looked after the wounded prince, and his rapid recovery immediately raised the profile of nurse training. One of the nurses, Haldane Turiff, was recruited to be the first Matron at the new Alfred Hospital in Melbourne.

Over the following decade, nurse-training programs commenced at the Alfred Hospital, the Melbourne Hospital for Sick Children, and the Melbourne Hospital, but there was no agreed standard of training. Springy proposed the formation of the Victorian Trained Nurses Association 'to improve and protect nursing by registering trained nurses, to introduce a uniform curriculum of training and examination, to look after the welfare of nurses by establishing a benefit scheme and generally to promote the interests of nurses'.[5]

The VTNA's inaugural meeting was held at the Melbourne Hospital on 19 April 1901, and the first council was elected on 12 June. Under Springy's presidency, membership was restricted to nurses who had undertaken three years of training at one of the hospitals endorsed by the VTNA. Additional training was encouraged in special areas, one of which was midwifery, recognised in 'special registration'. Of the thirty general nurses who were foundation signatories of the VTNA, seven also had midwifery endorsement: six from the Royal Women's Hospital in Melbourne and one from Queen Charlotte's Hospital in London.

The prefix 'Royal' was obtained for the VTNA by royal charter in 1904. The charter was sought at Springy's suggestion, after Queen Alexandra expressed interest in the work of nursing associations. Springy said, in a letter to matrons and training schools, that the uniform system of training and examinations had been 'so generally satisfactory that the Association has had the title "Royal" conferred on it by His Most Gracious Majesty, King Edward VII'.[6]

The battle for improved standards of care was fought on many fronts, and none was more contentious than midwifery. Opinion was divided on what midwifery entailed: some took the view that in the great majority of cases, highly skilled nursing was unnecessary, leaving plenty of time for domestic work, which would enable the mother to rest and thus regain her health. The fees of a general nurse would be an unnecessary expense when lesser training would do. Hence, specific midwifery training without general nursing training would be a much more economical option.[7] The alternative view was that skilled care was required to reduce maternal and infant illness and death. The public needed to differentiate between nursing and household work, and understand that having trained nurses do domestic chores demeaned the profession.

Springy was strongly on the side of professionalism. For a time, the Women's Hospital accepted the RVTNA's standards, but found it increasingly difficult to recruit enough trainees to cope with its workload. The Australian Trained Nurses Association, which had hitherto been unsuccessful in persuading Victoria to affiliate, endorsed midwifery-only training as an economical compromise, and in 1905 the Women's Hospital reinstated midwifery training for fresh practitioners who were not trained nurses. However, the RVTNA representatives declined to sign those certificates, significantly diminishing the status of the qualification.

As public disquiet with nursing's 'Sarah Gamps' (the stereotype of a slovenly, untrained and incompetent nurse) fuelled debate over appropriate qualifications, proposals were made for the regulation of midwifery. The Medical Society of Victoria Puerperal Sepsis Subcommittee reported in 1905 that untrained midwives ignored surgical cleanliness and predisposed women to preventable sickness. It opposed legislation for the registration of midwives on the grounds that this would legitimise inadequately trained practitioners, who would fail to call on doctors. Springy added his opinion that the majority of midwives registered under such legislation in England were trained to an exceedingly low level and 'were not fit to attend

Australian blacks' – a racist insult against Aboriginal people as much as a slur against the midwives.[8]

In June 1905, Springy, in his role as president of the RVTNA, wrote to all the registered nurse training schools in the state, thanking them for their cooperation in standardising nursing training across Victoria, and advising that there was now also a statewide educational standard for matrons, which would become compulsory in three years' time.[9] The initiatives of the Australasian Trained Nurses Association were successfully adopted, and members of the profession expressed their gratitude for Springy's contribution by presenting him with a set of fifty bound volumes of standard works of literature. In his letter of thanks, he referred to his efforts as 'a labour of love undertaken on behalf of Victorian nursing'.[10]

Although nursing was not to become a university course for another hundred years, university training for physiotherapy (then known as 'massage') began much earlier.[11] In his lectures to medical students from 1886, Springy had spoken of its beneficial effects and 'its power for evil if ignorantly applied'.[12] In his textbook, he said that physiotherapists 'cured problems by increasing circulation, strengthening muscles, breaking down adhesions, improving metabolism, affecting the nervous system, and restoring symmetrical and normal development, while medicine simply waited for nature to heal'.[13] He applauded 'the greatness of physiotherapy's service to medicine'.[14]

Small societies of masseurs had formed in Victoria, New South Wales and South Australia around the turn of the century. In 1905, a meeting was convened in Melbourne to discuss forming a national association. The instigators were Mr Teepoo Hall and Springy, who chaired the meeting.[15] This led to the founding of the Australian Massage Association in February 1906, and training associated with universities began in Melbourne in 1906, Sydney in 1907, and Adelaide in 1908.[16] Students completed a two-year full-time diploma, in which they studied anatomy, physiology and natural philosophy (physics) alongside medical students. Physiotherapy subjects were taught by specialised medical and experienced physiotherapy practitioners, and supervised clinical practice occurred in university hospitals.

The Australian Massage Association benefited greatly, both in practical measures and in prestige, from the patronage of significant medical figures such as Springthorpe. The Association set standards for education, ethical behaviour, and clinical practice. Many existing massage practitioners upgraded their qualifications, and the Association conducted monthly lectures.

Springy was also influential in supporting physiotherapy at the Melbourne Hospital. The chief physiotherapist taught students for four decades in the hospital's new Lonsdale Street premises, where Springthorpe had helped secure 'a generous Massage department'.[17] He continued as one of the guiding figures of the Australian Massage Association, using his connections and voice to pursue registration under an Act of Parliament.[18] By 1914, Australia was the only country in which physiotherapy education in the biomedical sciences was at university level.[19]

Springy strongly advocated for physiotherapy throughout his life. His interest in it seems linked to his appreciation of sporting activity. Even though his cycling days were over, he continued his involvement on the administrative side. A 1905, a newspaper reported:

> The annual invitation championship meeting of the Melbourne Amateur Wheelers' Club was held this afternoon on the Exhibition Arena ... During the afternoon the Lieutenant-Governor, Sir John Madden, visited the arena and was received by the president, Dr Springthorpe, and the honorary secretary, Mr E.J. Matlock. After watching several races Sir John was entertained by the committee. Dr Springthorpe proposed 'Renewed health and continued prosperity to His Excellency' who, he said, had at great personal sacrifice given encouragement to amateur athletics, and by his attendance at the meeting put heart into the Melbourne Amateur Wheelers.[20]

Dentistry was another special area of interest for Springy. A group of dentists had formed the Odontological Society of Victoria in 1884, to achieve meaningful training within and regulation of the profession. John Iliffe, a member of the Odontological Society who later became its president, was the driving force behind those negotiations.

From the time of his return from England in 1883, Springy had supported the movement. Because of his university post and prominence in medical politics, he was appointed as a member of the Dental Board of Victoria in 1888, later becoming its chairman.

He supported Iliffe's work in founding the Melbourne Dental Hospital in 1890 and was influential in the subsequent development of the Australian College of Dentistry in 1897. In 1904, discussions between the University of Melbourne and the Dental Board of Victoria culminated in a recommendation that a dental faculty be established at the university. This was approved, the College of Dentistry thus becoming affiliated with the university, and Springy was elected as inaugural dean of the new faculty.[21] Initially, there was a two-year diploma, qualifying the candidate for membership of the Australian College of Dentistry. Subsequently, the curriculum was extended, leading to the establishment of the LDS (Licentiate of Dental Surgery) in 1898, the Bachelor of Dental Surgery in 1904 and the Doctor of Dental Science in 1911, conferred for the first time in 1913.[22]

At its annual dinner on 7 December 1904, the Dental Students' Society proposed a toast to Springy in his role as president of the Dental Board.

In response, Springy said that as an examiner he knew that the students were worthy of the recognition they were now receiving. The standards were as good as those in England and the USA and were now acknowledged in Australia. Dental students were thus an independent part of the University and the Dental Board had requested professional registration. When this was granted, the graduates would become entitled to practice in any part of the British Empire. His response was loudly applauded.[23]

The Argus newspaper later eulogised:

> It was largely due to the efforts of Dr. Springthorpe that the profession of dentistry was raised to a definite status in Victoria. Until about 1890 any man who could pull a tooth was able to obtain registration as a dentist. As the leader from that date of a movement which resulted in the foundation of the Australian College of Dentistry in Melbourne, as president of the Dental Board for 13 years, and as dean of the Faculty of Dentistry at the University of Melbourne for 10 years, he was identified with every movement for the improvement of the status of dentists.[24]

In 1902, Springy's younger brother Frederick died, at the age of just forty-five.[25] Frederick lived in Gordon, a northern suburb of Sydney, worked as an importer in the city,[26] and in 1897 had been appointed a justice of the peace and honorary magistrate.[27] The funeral, which Springy attended, took place at the parish church, with the Reverend L. S. Thomas officiating.[28]

Springy's father, John Springthorpe, died of prostate cancer on 27 February 1906. He was buried at the Lee cemetery in Kent on Saturday 3 March. Travel times did not enable Springy's attendance, but the event was recorded in his diary without further comment.

Springy continued his busy schedule of lectures, medical work, and organisational commitments. He had given a lecture on medical therapeutics to the Royal Victorian Trained Nurses Association on 19 April 1905, and the annual lecture to the Medical Students' Society, titled 'Some wonder voyages of the ego', in Wilson Hall at Melbourne University in July 1905. He arranged for both of these to be published by Sands and McDougall so that they would be available to the public. Such behaviour attracted criticisms of self-aggrandisement, but the satirical weekly *Punch* made light of it:

> Some small people seem to be packed with compressed energy. They seem to bounce through the world like a ping-pong ball, which is the most resilient object which Science has yet invented. Their ceaseless vitality is irritating to longer and more lethargic men, who always are glad of an opportunity to call them by nasty names ... It takes energy to devote yourself to half-a-dozen things outside your ordinary work, even though your devotion to them brings its own reward in frequent publication of your name. So the medical man who holds more variety of offices than most of his professional brethren must naturally be known as Springy ... The little round doctor holds many degrees. He is an M.A., and an M.D., and an M.R.C.P. And he holds more offices. He is an honorary physician at the Melbourne Hospital ... he is lecturer at the Melbourne University ... he is president of the Dental Board of Victoria, and has done an immense amount to make dentistry the science which it is in this State today ... he is president of the Royal Victorian Trained Nurses' Association—more than president, he is dictator and sovereign lord of it, and the nurses swear by him. Moreover, as everybody has lately realised, he

is one of the official visitors to the metropolitan lunatic asylums. Columns of newspaper print, with his name at the foot, recently placed him before the public, as the one untiring champion of improvement and reform. Students, dentists and nurses all swear by Springthorpe's name. We can leave it at that.[29]

One of Springy's main areas of practice was with epilepsy. His early training at the National Hospital for Diseases of the Nervous System in Queen Square, London, had introduced him to the latest conceptualisations and treatments of the disorder. In particular, the teachings of Dr John Hughlings Jackson had great significance for him. Jackson postulated that most seizures began in the cerebral cortex, and that seizure activity would produce clinical signs related to that region of the brain. He introduced the concept of focal epilepsy with localised seizure activity, in contrast to the generalised major seizures. Although most attention has historically been given to major seizures, about ninety per cent of incident cases in adults involve focal seizures.

As various parts of the cerebral cortex subserve different roles, the specific pattern of abnormal brain activity reflects the location of its source. Knowing the location of the abnormal focus has great significance for understanding the underlying brain pathology and for possible treatments, such as brain surgery. However, in Springthorpe's time, the available treatments were limited, and the improving diagnostic accuracy was merely one more step in the scientific medical journey.

Springy collected data on his epilepsy cases, and in 1886 presented the results to a meeting of the Medical Society of Victoria. His descriptions indicated a predominance of focal seizures. Before presenting his data in the form of detailed tabulation, he briefly described current concepts of the pathophysiology, including Hughlings Jackson's new theory of the role of the cerebral cortex. His table covered a range of factors then thought to cause seizures (although many have subsequently been discounted). One of those factors was 'peripheral irritants'. The concept was that a trigger message from a source outside the central nervous system would prompt over-excitable cells in the brain to ignite seizure activity. While bromide sedatives could dampen the brain's excitability, removal of the irritant might prevent or reduce seizure activity.[30]

In the following year, Springy delivered another epilepsy paper, this time specifically on the elimination of peripheral irritants.[31] He classified them into four groups: ovarian and uterine irritants; intestinal worms in children; 'gastric irritation' (indigestion and liver disorder, which included obesity associated with excessive alcohol intake); and centric irritants, which included anxiety and overwork.

A further year later, in 1888, he presented the third paper in his trilogy: 'Notes on fifty cases of epilepsy'.[32] He noted that nearly half of the cohort had a family history of epilepsy and more than half had experienced onset before adulthood. Many of the cases were what was then referred to as *'petit mal'* (transiently impaired conscious state without convulsions). One of this paper's aims was to respond to criticisms of earlier papers that the follow-up time was too short to reach conclusions about the course of the disorder or its response to treatment. To requests that he explain his treatment methods, Springy listed the following steps:

> Firstly, the removal of the previously mentioned peripheral irritants. In the case of focal seizures, the application of a ligature around the affected limb as a counter-irritant to that at the source. Secondly, the administration of potassium bromide, beginning with 30 grains at night and tailoring the dosage as required. If this is insufficient, the addition of zinc oxide, belladonna, cannabis indica or digitalis may be trialled. In the case of 'petit mal' the use of caffeine and nitroglycerine were indicated. Finally, according to Dr Wilks of London, 'A seton set in the nape of the neck should never be forgotten'.[33]

The eminent Melbourne neurologist Peter Bladin commented recently on this:

> This is a mix of very old and reasonably new treatments; but the idea of using a seton—a skein of silk sutures threaded through the loose skin at the back of the neck to create chronic weeping suppuration—is something out of the Middle Ages!
>
> Overall, Springthorpe's paper paints a good picture of the clinical concepts in this transition period from old to modern epileptology. But his most important message was

the importance of considering this clinical and social problem as a subject for detailed discussion by all concerned with the management of people suffering from epilepsy ... Primitive though it was, the treatment of epilepsy in Victoria in the 19th century was in line with that used in most countries.[34]

As well as having a frightening appearance in public, major epileptic seizures usually led to unemployability and often to destitution and admission to mental asylums. The 1886 Zox Commission enquiring into these institutions reported that many patients with epilepsy were inappropriately detained, simply because there was nowhere else to provide more appropriate treatment.[35] This problem did not exist only in Australia. In 1893, an important report by London's Charity Organisation Society, 'The Epileptic and Crippled Child and Adult', described what should be done.

In 1903, the National Council of Women of Victoria (NCWV), founded in 1902, held its first congress. Dr Mary Page Stone, one of the first women graduates of the University of Melbourne Medical School, presented a paper titled 'Epileptic colonies', which made such an impression on the audience that they decided to advocate founding a colony-farm for people with epilepsy. Springy and his colleague John Fishbourne were asked to lend professional assistance and explain to the NCWV what was needed to set up such colony-farms. Lady Margaret Talbot, wife of the newly arrived governor of Victoria, was recruited to the cause by the president of the NCWV, Lady Janet Clarke. This gave the group enough influence to launch a public appeal and approach the premier, Sir Thomas Bent, with a direct request for public funding. Springy threw himself into the campaign, writing a string of letters to newspapers, such as the following in August 1905:

TO THE EDITOR OF THE ARGUS.

Sir,—The public has but to learn what a far- reaching and terrible evil epilepsy really is in order to give the Lady Talbot Fund that support and sympathy which it so thoroughly deserves.

Epilepsy is not simply a horrible case of fits. The sudden and unavoidable loss of consciousness makes places, times, and events, which are usually harmless to others, sources of danger and even death to the epileptic. Without warning they fall in front of trains and trams, down stairs, off ladders, into the fire, and are suffocated, drowned, or otherwise injured. Thus, out of every eight epileptics two carry scars, one has marks of burns, one dies of accident, and two during a series of fits. Nor is the disease one which they can avoid. On the contrary, it is mainly an inherited weakness, lit up by strain and stress, that aren't harmless to us, their more fortunate brothers and sisters. Think of it! Out of every four cases one occurs in little children under five, one-half in children under ten, and three quarters under twenty years of age, mainly through no fault of their own!

Nor does this complete the picture. There is much more infinitely worse. The epileptic child is sent back from school, cannot mix with his fellows, has practically no amusements, grows up solitary, introspective, and uneducated. The epileptic young man or woman drifts on without interest; or occupation, a personal failure, a family burden. Some saddened and despondent relative, generally the mother or sister, heroically takes up a lifelong burden of servitude. For the epileptic, no school, no social intercourse, no work, no play, no career, but failure, neglect, dementia, despair. And for his attendant a wearing sorrow, a life's sacrifice illumined by a ray of hope. What a difference in the Epileptic Colony? There these unfortunates lead an outdoor life—upon a farm, under supervision and sympathetic treatment. They find a home, a school, a career, occupation, and social intercourse. Their seizures are much less severe and not half as frequent, and, outside their attacks, they live, walk, and enjoy themselves much the same as ordinary folk. From England, Europe and America comes the same tale of satisfactory results, and the same rush for new colonies and additional inmates.

The present attempt is based upon the same satisfactory lines. The proposed colony will be open to all, full pay, half pay, or no pay, in proportion to its limits in accommodation and maintenance. The Government has done its share in providing the ground, £3,000 in money, and a yearly grant for the poorer cases. The National Council of Women has made it their inaugural and memorial effort, and Lady Talbot has given it not only the sanction of her name, but her warm and strenuous support.

And as its great and lasting benefits become recognised, it must commend itself to all sections of the community as an act of humanity to deplorable sufferers, as a matter of state and individual economy, as a means of freeing many afflicted households from an almost intolerable burden, and as the scientific and only successful way of treating epileptics as a class. In such a case it is the large number of small contributions that will help even more than the small number of large ones.

Yours &c.,

Aug. 3. J.W. SPRINGTHORPE.[36]

Lady Talbot was a most effective campaigner, and 19 July 1906 saw the passage of legislation establishing the Talbot Colony for Epileptics. A mixture of public and private funding had given the project a strong financial foundation, and a Mr James Mason donated 'Masonmeadows', his 165-acre property in Clayton, as the site of the colony-farm.

Figure 20: 'Masonmeadows'

The Talbot Colony was officially opened by the Governor of Victoria, Sir Reginald Talbot, in 1907, shortly before he and Lady Margaret returned to England.

Springy was on the management committee from the outset and remained actively involved in the colony's administration, and in the treatment of its inmates, for the next twenty-five years. He often referred patients for admission from his private practice, as well as from the Melbourne Hospital. He viewed the colony as a refuge that was to be made as homely as possible. It was not to be a place of detention, or even of work, though farm work offered the opportunity for healthy, productive occupation. He saw it as a kind of convalescent home from which residents might return to their own home, or to other activities, when ready. He acknowledged that some might find other forms of occupation more appropriate.

As modern treatments for epilepsy became more effective, the colony broadened its role to include brain injury rehabilitation. In 1958, it received a 'Royal' appellation in its title. When Monash University occupied the site in 1961, the organisation relocated to the Chandler Highway edge of Yarra Bend Park and changed its name to Royal Talbot Rehabilitation Centre. In 1988, it became part of the Austin Health Network where it continues its traditional work but with a wider range of brain-injured patients.

Springy had similar humanitarian views about the administration of mental hospitals. From early in his career he had been critical of their restrictiveness, poor quality of care and poor training of staff, and in 1901 he was appointed as one of the Official Visitors to asylums. Soon afterwards, he was drawn into a dispute with serious political ramifications, which was covered extensively in the newspapers.

Reports say that, early in the year, an asylum medical officer had sent a patient out to buy liquor for him, which he then consumed. He was observed to be drunk on duty, following which he took sedative drugs and went absent without leave. He was subsequently found in a private hospital under treatment for 'an acute alcoholic outbreak', and was granted three months' leave of absence on full pay to recover, on the understanding that he would not resume his work.[37] On the expiry of that recovery period, the inspector-general of asylums, Dr M'Creery, discovered that the medical officer had transferred to another asylum to resume work.

Dr M'Creery submitted a report to the Chief Secretary of Victoria, Mr John Murray, stating that the man was unfit for the position. However, Murray, who himself had overcome alcohol problems, had assured the man that when he recovered, he would be re-employed. Murray disregarded M'Creery's report. M'Creery protested, and Murray requested two of the three official visitors to asylums, Drs Jamieson and Joske, report on the medical officer's fitness for duty. The report is said to have recommended that he not be employed at a Melbourne asylum, but that he might be able to undertake a less demanding role at a country asylum. Murray ignored the report and directed that the man be employed in Melbourne.[38]

M'Creery threatened to resign, and refused to re-employ the man without a written directive, though he reluctantly complied when he received one. He went on sick leave, and the superintendent of Kew Asylum, Dr William Beattie-Smith, became acting inspector-general of asylums. Only at this stage did Beattie-Smith become aware of the previous correspondence about the case. The medical officer had been appointed to work at Kew. Beattie-Smith, too, told Murray that the man was unfit for duty. He is reported to have said, 'Either he goes, or I will.'[39]

In the meantime, Springy, the third of the official visitors and the only one who had not been previously involved, had instituted his own enquiry under the Lunacy Statute, which gave him as an official visitor the power to compel anyone to testify, upon pain of a £50 fine.[40] He summonsed his two fellow official visitors, Drs Jamieson and Joske, as well as the medical officer in question and other hospital staff. The medical officer was represented by a lawyer, and it was a hostile process all round.

Murray refused to provide a copy of the official visitors' report, claiming that he had 'made full inquiries into, and finally dealt with, the matter'. Jamieson and Joske also refused to provide their report, refused to give sworn evidence, and objected to Springy's characterisation of their involvement. Springy had said that they 'saw fit to flout my authority, to impute motives, and to intimidate witnesses'.[41]

The medical officer at the heart of the case declined to answer questions on the grounds that the matter had been dealt with by Murray and that, as a public servant under Murray, he should not express approval or disapproval of that judgment. Springy questioned a few of the hospital staff and called Dr Fishbourne as an expert witness on the management of lunatic asylums. Fishbourne 'condemned as subversive of discipline and injurious to the welfare of the institution the reinstatement of the doctor in question'.[42]

Springy forwarded his report to Murray, but before it was even seen, Murray announced that he had accepted Beattie-Smith's resignation. This prompted a wave of correspondence to newspapers and appeals to government, which stated that the loss of Beattie-Smith would be a tragedy for the mental health system.[43] The incident also prompted newspaper commentary about serious deficiencies in Victoria's mental hospitals and the need for 'lunacy reform'.[44]

Springy's report outlined the events and stated that 'the medical officer is now on duty as the senior medical officer at the asylum, without any loss of status or other punishment'. He went on to say:

> Misconduct and habits such as have been proved in this case must lower the tone of asylum administration, render a medical officer unreliable in duty and unfit to exercise discipline. No such officer, especially if he has similarly broken down previously, should be in dispensary charge, with uncontrolled daily access to drugs and drink, or in any circumstances in medical charge of such patients as the insane, who have no voice for reason or complaint. The one position which should be absolutely closed to such a man should be that of medical officer to an asylum. The only other medical officer who in my recollection has been convicted of drunkenness in a Victorian asylum was dismissed [from] the service.[45]

In response to his two fellow official visitors' lack of cooperation with his enquiry, Springy asked Murray to 'bring their conduct under the notice of the Governor in Council'. He stated that Beattie-Smith 'was perfectly justified in refusing to accept the responsibility of working with a colleague whose unfitness was proved', and then went on to attack Murray's position directly:

> The Chief Secretary certainly had asked the acting superintendent to formulate a charge, but it was absurd to do that in face of the fact that the Chief Secretary had already stated that he had made 'full inquiry' into the case, and had 'finally dealt' with

it. The absurdity and seriousness of the present situation was accentuated by the fact that if Mr Beattie-Smith resigns, the position so vacated by him of medical superintendent [of the Kew asylum] will be filled by the medical officer in question, as he is next in seniority. If others decline to take the responsibility of Inspector under Mr Murray's administration, this officer may even become the professional head of the department, and affairs may thus be left in the hands of incompetents and derelicts.[46]

But Murray held his ground, and Dr Beattie-Smith resigned as superintendent of the Kew asylum.[47] This did not solve the government's problem, however, as it was further embarrassed by strong criticisms of asylums. *The Age* newspaper said that the incident revealed the need for 'drastic reform in the general management of hospitals in this State and for the introduction of modern methods of treating the inmates'. It detailed significant structural and professional shortcomings, including overcrowded conditions, out-of-date buildings, and inadequate sanitation, ventilation and lighting. Staff were poorly trained and qualified, and there was no differentiation in treatment for different disorders or degrees of illness. The government was not spared, either: 'The necessity for reorganisation has been urged upon successive Governments during the past twenty years, but the unfortunate lunatics as a class have no friends— being voteless they have, to say the least, no political friends— and have fallen on unheeding ears'.[48]

A bill was quickly drafted to relieve the pressure. This provided private treatment for those who could afford it, in place of care at an asylum. It also instated measures to avoid sending people in an acute mental state to gaol, and created a Lunacy Board to manage the entire system, reporting directly to parliament, which was thus independent of the government of the day. *The Age* concluded: 'If Mr Murray would pass this bill there would be an end probably to the scandals that have disgraced our management of the insane'.[49]

Unwilling to be the scapegoats for the asylums' appalling conditions, attendants issued their own pamphlet on lunacy reform and the shortcomings of the medical staff in charge. They claimed that doctors spent so much of their time 'attending to details of domestic management, the control of the gardens and farms, the purchase of stock, and, indeed, every aspect of asylum life' that they did not give time to classifying patients like asylums in other parts of the world. The doctors gave most of their attention to treatment of physical illnesses, and until this changed, patients' mental illnesses would continue to be neglected.[50]

As would happen repeatedly during his career, Springy's forthright approach led to division and acrimony between members of his own profession. Drs Jamieson and Joske recommended a properly conducted enquiry, because the purpose of Springy's 'was not so much to inquire as to convict'.[51] An enquiry was also demanded by Dr Stuart Macbirnie, who identified himself as the medical officer in question.[52] Mr Murray announced that he had already decided to appoint a board that would inquire into the lunatic asylums' management. But *The Age* was far from pleased with his handling of the affair, which was hotly debated in parliament. The newspaper accused him of:

> vulgar abuse of Dr Springthorpe, whom he accused of craving notoriety, and Dr Beattie- Smith, whom he described as a sort of physical and mental degenerate, almost as eccentric as his insane patients.
>
> This attack on men who could not defend themselves was warmly resented by the House, Sir Alexander Peacock protesting strongly against the Chief Secretary's language. Both Mr. Murray and the Premier made it clear that a full investigation would be made into asylum administration.[53]

The Age subsequently opined: 'If the MacBirnie incident, Dr. Springthorpe's somewhat theatrical action and Dr. Beattie-Smith's resignation lead up to a thorough reform in our lunacy system, the public will have cause to rejoice over all of them.'[54] One week later, the government (which was a minority one) was outvoted on a procedural matter and unexpectedly called a snap election on 1 October. The government improved its position but was again a minority, holding just forty-seven seats out of ninety-five.

The board of enquiry reported three weeks later, finding that Dr Macbirnie was unfit for duty on the evening specified, but that there was no evidence this was caused by excessive alcohol. He did absent himself from the asylum, but his state of health appears to have necessitated this. He was therefore exonerated from the charges. The government election had taken attention away from the scandal, but when Dr M'Creery, who'd returned to work as Inspector of Asylums, presented his annual report to parliament, it acknowledged that the criticisms had been heard, and enumerated a program of reform 'to bring our asylums up to a proper modern standard'. This included establishing a hospital for acute cases, removing three hundred chronic patients from Kew, making structural changes to the Kew building, increasing medical and nursing staff numbers, providing better selection of and training for attendants and nurses, and enacting administrative reforms to achieve greater accountability – free of political influence.[55]

Over a year later, the government brought forward the *Lunacy Act 1903*, which established the new Lunacy Department and implemented the changes that Springy and Beattie-Smith had been advocating.[56] Needless to say, they were not thanked for their role. Beattie-Smith worked thereafter in private practice, though he continued to be an influential voice in medical politics and mental health training. Springy continued his outspoken criticisms, prompting a later mental health reformer, Dr Eric Cunningham Dax, to observe: 'Between 1885 and 1910 Springthorpe had a vast influence for good upon the mental health services'. He had exposed the 'dreadful conditions and restraints in the asylums and greatly influenced the promulgation of the 1903 Lunacy Act'. Indeed, Cunningham Dax dubbed Springthorpe 'one of the greatest medical reformers in Victoria'.[57]

In the midst of his involvement with masseurs, nurses, dentists and a range of other committees, Springy found time to convene a small group of University of Melbourne staff to discuss the process of selecting Rhodes Scholars from Victoria. Included in his list of publications is 'Chairman's Address—The Cecil Rhodes Bequest—Melbourne', giving the false impression that he was chair of the committee making the awards. In fact, Springy's committee sent its report to the official university committee chaired by the governor of Victoria, Sir Reginald Talbot, and including the chancellor, Mr Frank Tate, and the professor of education, Baldwin Spencer.[58]

Having been on the St John Ambulance Association Council for just over ten years, Springy was elected chairman in 1907. His old mentors,

James Edward Neild and Henry Martyn Andrew, had both died, but he had several other close friends on the council. Dr William Snowball, the first trained paediatrician in Australia, and Dr Dan Gresswell, the Victorian Government's chief health officer (with whom Springy had campaigned against tuberculosis), had both been on the council for several years. They had been joined in 1903 by Surgeon-Major George Horne, who had then been in charge of the medical militia at Victoria Barracks (and later became Victoria's first St John Ambulance Brigade Commissioner), and by Surgeon-General Sir William Williams, the first Commonwealth Government Chief Health Officer and the first person in Victoria to be invested as a Knight of St John (in 1904). The St John Ambulance Council was a very powerful group in those days.

One of Springy's first tasks as chairman of St John Council was planning the visit to Melbourne of Theodore Roosevelt's Great White Fleet in 1908. The fleet was on a world tour to demonstrate that the United States of America was now a naval superpower, capable of putting fleets wherever they may be needed around the world. Only seven years after Federation and the opening of the Australian Parliament in Melbourne, Prime Minister Andrew Fisher was keen to foster a connection with the new potential ally, rather than remain totally dependent on Great Britain. A state visit was proposed. Sixteen American battleships steamed into Port Phillip Bay and anchored at Port Melbourne. On Saturday 29 August 1908, three thousand American sailors marched an eight-kilometre route from Port Melbourne to the city to receive a civic welcome. The public response was sensational: half of Melbourne's one-million population turned out to see the march.

Until this time, Victoria had no public first aid capability and only a rudimentary professional ambulance service. St John had been offering public classes in first aid since 1883, and there were many certificate-holders but no membership organisation.

The professional ambulance service comprised a small number of horse-drawn ambulances run by St John from stables in the central city, Ascot Vale to the north-west, and Prahran to the south-east, together with a few Ashford litters (stretchers on wheels) located at police stations around the city. This would've been totally inadequate for a crowd of nearly half a million people, spread along a route extending some eight kilometres.

During the great event, Surgeon-Major George Horne was responsible for public safety. A small number of his militia men at Victoria Barracks had equipment, but he needed many more first-aiders. Being an honorary lecturer for St John, Horne knew that there were many people sufficiently trained to undertake the task, so he called for St John certificate-holders to volunteer. He received enough response to enable sixteen first-aid posts to be set up between Port Melbourne and the city. On the Fleet's march day, his First Aid Volunteers' Association treated five hundred casualties, prompting the St John council to declare the service such a success that it must be maintained. The council wrote to England for permission to begin a branch of the St John Ambulance Brigade in Melbourne. The branch officially began in 1910 and has continued ever since.

In 1909, Springy was succeeded as chairman by Dr Charles Bage, elevated to president and admitted as an Associate of the Order of St John. In 1912, he was promoted to Knight of Grace in the Order of St John, the second person in Victoria to be so honoured. He remained president until 1916.

Figure 21: Dr John Springthorpe KStJ

It was during Springy's term of office that St John bought its first motor ambulance, triggering a financial crisis, as the costs were not met by voluntary donations. This led to St John forming the Victorian Civil Ambulance Service, a corporate organisation able to charge fees to recover its costs, and thereby saving St John Ambulance from imminent bankruptcy.

Melbourne's first motor ambulance 1910

Civil ambulance service 1916

Figure 22: Melbourne's early motor ambulances

In 1908, Lancelot Springthorpe was partway through his studies at the University of Melbourne, receiving second-class honours in physics and chemistry.[59] The following year, Springy moved house. A horticulturist friend, Margaret Tuckett, and her husband decided to subdivide and sell their property, Omama Gardens, in Murrumbeena. This was still a semi-rural area, some thirteen kilometres south-east of Melbourne and not far from the Talbot Epileptic Colony at Clayton. Omama Gardens was well known, because it was the subject of Tuckett's widely read book *A Year in My Garden*. Springthorpe bought the house and garden and two adjoining blocks, totalling 4.5 acres (1.82 hectares).[60] He named it 'Joyous Gard', after Sir Lancelot's castle in the Arthurian legend.

Springy and the three children moved into Joyous Gard in December 1909. He had employed a housekeeper, Mrs Jessie Louise Johnstone, who served as house mother. She had come with her family from Tasmania a few years earlier. Her daughter, Daisie, was a nurse in Springy's medical practice.

Enid and Lancelot, who by this time had been living with their grandparents for more than twelve years, did not cope well with the transition to living with their father and his assertive personality. In 1910, the nineteen-year-old Lancelot ran away. He was missing for more than a year, much to Springy's anguish, before he finally wrote that he was working on a property in the Darling Downs in Queensland and did not intend to return. He remained estranged from his father for the rest of his life. (Lance was 'on the land' in Queensland for many years. He enlisted in the military in September 1913 – at which time he was working as an auctioneer at Goomeri – and died in Sydney on 4 March 1976.) Springy's younger son, Guy, who had been living not far away with his aunt Florence and thus had seen a lot more of his father, fared much better. He was still attending Trinity Grammar School in Kew, along with his second cousin, Martin Boyd. Guy went on to university and became a psychiatrist, reflecting his father's preoccupation with psychological medicine, while Martin Boyd went on to become a renowned writer and poet.

In 1910, when Melbourne Hospital renovated, its management presented to Springthorpe the old, magnificent entrance gates. These were installed at Joyous Gard.[61] Springthorpe was very proud of the garden, which had been laid out by Mrs Tuckett with the help of William Guilfoyle, and spent much of his time in later years tending to it. He described it as 'an old-fashioned garden, a landscape garden, and we do not bother about annuals at all—saves a lot of work, and to my mind is much more beautiful. We have quantities of flowers all the year round.'[62] He also placed in it the two sculptures by Web Gilbert that he had commissioned in 1910 for the garden around Annie's tomb.

Figure 23: Joyous Gard

In 1913, Arthur and Emma Minnie Boyd purchased blocks abutting Joyous Gard for their son Merric. They called it 'Open Country'. Merric suffered from epilepsy, and as Springy was the family physician and an expert in epilepsy, living next door seemed a good idea. After Merric married artist Doris Gough in 1915, their parents bought further properties on either side of Open Country, forming an artist's community, in which the couple's children, Arthur, David, Guy, Lucy and Mary Boyd, grew up.[63]

Springy's dedication to the University of Melbourne was unwavering. From 1911, he participated in a series of meetings to design a new medical curriculum, notwithstanding that a previous attempt at revision had not been adopted. The 1911 committee included clinical teachers such as Henry Maudsley, Richard Stawell, George Rennie, John Wilkinson, James Barrett, George Syme, Thomas Dunhill and Frederick Bird, and their determination led to success.[64]

In 1911, Springy attended the Australasian Medical Congress in Sydney, to which such luminaries as Sigmund Freud, Carl Jung and

Havelock Ellis sent papers to be read. Springy was deeply impressed by the psychotherapeutic approach, although sceptical of the importance the theory placed on unconscious sexual conflicts in neurosis. He gave greater weight to the effects of constitutional factors and other life events. Nevertheless, he advocated the inclusion of psychological medicine as a major component of medical student teaching and hospital practice.

In 1914, as Europe was plunging into war, Springy published his two-volume *Therapeutics, Dietetics and Hygiene: An Australian Text-Book*.[65] It was a great success and was immediately adopted as the textbook for his course at the University of Melbourne.

In writing his textbook, Springy took great pride in the role of tribal elder initiating a new generation into his way of thinking. He dedicated his book to 'My Alma Mater, My Old Hospital, and My Twelve Hundred Students 1887–1914'. In the book he referred to some of his other publications, one of which gave important context for his views. This was the Melbourne Hospital Inaugural Lecture of 1890. Springy had been called upon to deliver the second of these annual lectures to new student doctors. The first one, in the previous year, had been delivered by one of the senior surgeons, and the two streams (surgery and medicine) would alternate.[66]

Springy began his lecture by describing the evolution of the hospital clinical school. In the twenty-five years since 1865, when the University of Melbourne's first student doctors began their studies, there had been two hundred and thirty-nine graduates, many of whom later occupied positions of great importance. By 1890, the number of graduates had increased from three or four to about twenty each year.[67] He compared the Melbourne Hospital's clinical school favourably with the benchmark schools in London and Edinburgh. This was due in no small measure to the hospital school's affiliation with the University of Melbourne, which retained complete control over the non-clinical parts of its course. Earlier clinical teaching had been restricted to particular units of the hospital, but with the new curriculum introduced in 1886, trainees gained access to all patients. Despite slight residual resistance from an old guard who preferred the apprenticeship model, this arrangement progressed in line with other important changes. Whereas surgical instruction had previously commenced before trainees knew anatomy, and medical instruction before they knew physiology, the new plan was for systematic instruction before clinical exposure. Two registrars, one for surgery and one for medicine, were appointed to supervise the students, and to ensure that hospital records were properly kept.

For the first time, Springy noted and welcomed the presence of women medical students, who were admitted to the University of Melbourne in 1887: 'Personally, I believe in the right of women to qualify themselves to undertake the work of our profession, and am glad that our University has thrown its medical course open to them'.[68]

All these developments occurred at the same time as proposals for rebuilding the hospital. Many advocated relocating it from its site on the northern edge of the city, bounded by Swanston, Lonsdale, Russell and Little Lonsdale Streets, to Parkville, near the university. Springy was one of those who opposed the move and advocated redevelopment on site. The new facility would have some four hundred beds and was to be 'built according to modern ideas'.[69]

Old Melbourne Hospital.

New Melbourne Hospital.

Figures 24 and 25: The old and new Melbourne Hospital

By the time his textbook was published in 1914, the rebuilding in Lonsdale Street was complete. During World War II, the American military forces built a hospital at the Parkville site, which became the Royal Melbourne Hospital after the war, leaving the old Melbourne Hospital to become the Queen Victoria Hospital.

5. Springy's Textbook

Although Springy had trained as a neurologist in addition to his general physician training, and also had a special interest in psychological medicine, remaining at the forefront of a wide range of medical and allied health fields was central to his self-image – restricting his practice to a specialty area was not to be contemplated. So too in his personal life: as an educated Victorian-era gentleman, Springy believed that it was his duty to be knowledgeable about the arts, about political and historical events, and especially about new scientific developments. He attended not only medical congresses but also those of the Australian Association for the Advancement of Science.

This Renaissance Man image was reflected in the numerous literary allusions sprinkled through his writing, and occasionally in specific admonitions. In his textbook, for instance, he wrote:

> The Best Physician must combine the philosopher and the moralist with the scientist. He must possess a wide knowledge of men and things, a many-sided culture, a strength founded on knowledge, and a sympathy at once boundless and bottomless. And his sufficient reward will be that he becomes the confidant, the restorer, and, at times, the saviour of many human lives.[1]

THERAPEUTICS, DIETETICS AND HYGIENE

AN AUSTRALIAN TEXT-BOOK

BY

JOHN WILLIAM SPRINGTHORPE

M.A., M.D. Melb., M.R.C.P. Lond.

SENIOR PHYSICIAN TO THE MELBOURNE HOSPITAL; LECTURER ON THERAPEUTICS, DIETETICS AND HYGIENE, AND DEAN OF THE FACULTY OF DENTISTRY IN THE UNIVERSITY OF MELBOURNE; PRESIDENT SECTION HYGIENE, A.A.A.S. (BRISBANE), 1895; AND I.M.C. (DUNEDIN), 1896;
FIRST PRESIDENT ROYAL VICTORIAN TRAINED NURSES' ASSOCIATION, AND AUSTRALASIAN MASSAGE ASSOCIATION;
OFFICIAL VISITOR METROPOLITAN ASYLUMS, VICTORIA;
AND
KNIGHT OF GRACE OF THE ORDER OF THE HOSPITAL OF ST. JOHN OF JERUSALEM IN ENGLAND.

WITH ILLUSTRATIONS.

VOL. I.—HYGIENE AND DIETETICS.

et scire semper et agere.

COPYRIGHT.

MELBOURNE:
PRINTED BY FORD & SON, DRUMMOND STREET, CARLTON.
PUBLISHED BY JAMES LITTLE, COLLINS STREET, MELBOURNE.

1914.

Figure 26: Textbook frontispiece

Early in the book, Springy discussed infections as a battle between organisms, then discussed parasitism and symbiosis. In considering the difficulties of eradicating infection by external organisms, he pondered whether the presence of those organisms might change physiology to 'offer a suitable soil for other organisms which at present are only "poor relations" and quite outside the pale of aggression. It is, indeed, questionable whether, in some form or other, parasitism and infectious diseases are not a property of life as we at present know it.'[2]

A century later, our studies of the microbiome would seem to bear that out. For instance, a recent article in *Scientific American* said:

> Scientists' rapidly expanding knowledge makes it clear that we are not made up primarily of 'human' cells that are occasionally invaded by microbes; our body is really a superorganism of cohabiting cells, bacteria, fungi and most numerous of all: viruses. The latest counts indicate that as much as half of all the biological matter in your body is not human. A decade ago researchers were barely aware that the human virome existed. Today we see the vast virome as an integral part of the larger human microbiome, a crazy quilt of passive and active microscopic organisms that occupy almost every corner of our being.[3]

Springy used imagery of soil widely through the book, not least in relation to tuberculosis:

> There is probably no subject in Anglo-Saxon medicine more important than that of strengthening the resisting power of the individual against 'the great white plague' of tuberculosis … An illuminating analogy is that of a seed, the soil, and the crop. The crop is consumption, the seed is the germ, and the soil is the individual constitution … just as the soil is the main factor, so individual constitution may make all the difference between susceptibility and immunity … Be healthy and you will not be consumptive.[4]

The germ theory of disease, competing with miasma, witchcraft and other explanations from antiquity, had been enthusiastically embraced by the medical profession since the pioneering work of Louis Pasteur in the 1850s. While he supported the advancing knowledge about bacteriology, Springy was slightly unusual in his emphasis on other factors that influenced how diseases manifested. He regarded the 'individual constitution' as predominantly inherited, although influenced by environmental factors. He advocated regular exercise, good food and a healthy lifestyle as important factors in strengthening it. Conversely, he argued that people who were 'constitutionally weak', had an 'ill-balanced temperament', or had inherited tendencies to disease were predisposed to ill-health. Nevertheless, he believed that constitutional weakness, though mainly inherited, could be exacerbated by poor food, exhaustion or over-emotionality, making the person susceptible to illnesses such as tuberculosis, syphilis and cancer. In Springy's view, 'The healthy resist disease'.[5]

The temperament 'types' – sanguine, nervous, hepatic and lymphatic – Springy attributed largely to heredity, although he stated they could also be influenced by lifestyle. The hepatic (a type characterised by obesity and a susceptibility to liver and kidney disease) he considered particularly subject to such influence. To him, recognition of this link was a crucial underpinning of the physician's education:

> We find mind and matter existing side by side and so interwoven that the physical affects the psychical, and the psychical affects the physical in a continuous series of interactions. You have thus as much need of psychology as of physiology— and yet to most of you the former is a quite unknown science.[6]

By 1914, Charles Darwin's theory of evolution by natural selection, published more than half a century earlier, was so well accepted in medical circles that it barely rated a mention in Springy's book. He made much more of later writings by Darwin's cousin, Francis Galton FRS (1822–1911). This extraordinary English scientist (statistician, sociologist, psychologist, anthropologist, eugenicist, meteorologist and psychometrician) was very active in the British Association for the Advancement of Science, presenting many papers on a variety of topics over a forty-year span. In meteorology, he devised the first weather map and proposed a theory of anticyclones. He created the statistical concepts of correlation and regression towards the mean. In his study of human differences, he studied the heritability and racial differences in fingerprints, identifying common patterns and devising a classification system that is still used in forensic science.[7]

Galton was the first to apply statistical methods to the study of human differences and inheritance of intelligence, founding the science of psychometrics. He coined the term 'eugenics' and the phrase 'nature versus nurture'. He did many studies on families over generations, especially twin studies, and concluded that the evidence favoured nature (heredity) rather than nurture (environment). He advocated for 'eugenic' marriages and providing incentives for such couples to have children. Springy was convinced of the heredity argument but was opposed to compulsory implementation of breeding control except in the case of gross abnormalities:

> We are indebted to Galton for the modern scientific conception, by which the breeding of human beings generally is to be placed on a scientific footing. This study he named 'Eugenics'. Every physician who has the welfare of his race at heart should do all in his power to learn its laws, and advance its claims in every reasonable and tactful manner. Interference with Nature's plan of natural selection, either positively by mating the fittest, or negatively by refusing or restricting to the unfit the right to propagate, is difficult, complex and even uncertain.[8]

Springy pointed out that many remarkable people came from unremarkable backgrounds, that many were in otherwise poor health, and equally that many impaired individuals came from seemingly good stock. He concluded that 'mating by natural preference will remain the main avenue to reproduction' but hoped that education would lead to voluntary reduction of risky inheritance. Sterilisation, in his view, should be 'reserved for certain definite cases and classes, which the widest and latest scientific investigations have unmistakably justified'. After all, for health, 'This is a matter, in the first place, of breeding'.[9]

Later in the book, however, he was not so deterministic about heredity: 'Of all the factors concerned in healthy development none is more important than food'. He wrote fifteen chapters on digestion, dietetics, the classification of foods, and the composition of diets – including portions, cooking and preservation. The chapter on the dietetics of infancy, youth and disease included variations for a huge number of different medical conditions, closing with notes about surgical cases, 'diet cures', and recipes for the sick room. This strong emphasis on diet was a little unusual for the time, but understandable because dietetics was part of Springy's brief as a university lecturer.[10]

Near the end of his book, Springy returned to his earlier theme of the importance of the mind:

> It will have become self-evident that, if we are to obtain the best results in promoting health and averting disease, we must go beyond those primarily physical conditions which are generally called treatment and include some systematic endeavour to influence the mind itself... Freud's psychoanalysis is a scientific detailed attempt to discover all the significant experiences and psychologically important motives and impulses from the earliest childhood, and to utilize these factors therapeutically— even dreams (? the fulfilment of unconscious wishes) are thus analysed ... in most cases, the partial and yet searching investigation which becomes the routine of experienced psychopathic practitioners will be sufficiently effective.[11]

Springy also argued that 'The first step is securing the patient's confidence' as a prelude to counselling, advice, suggestion and the rewarding of appropriate functional activities. Several of his other interests were noted: 'Although obscured by other areas of modern medicine, physiotherapy remains one of the greatest of remedial agents, especially with new scientific advances'. On the education of women, he wrote:

> The main interest of womanhood must ever remain the rearing of splendid children ... Nineteenth century education conceded to the girls equal education with her brother. This tends to make her an ineffective copy of a boy. Separation of the sexes would allow specialisation to suit girls, with 'domestic economy' made the central study, with training in the appreciation of beauty of outline, colour, design and ornament, so important to her future home life.[12]

On the education of people with disability, Springy wrote: 'For their own sakes, and for the sake of the community, they need special care and treatment. Moral, philosophical and religious principles should underpin schooling.'[13]

The textbook was, of course, written primarily for medical students. But many of the concepts he taught were also reproduced in papers to medical journals and presentations at congresses, which were then frequently reprinted as pamphlets. Springy was fond of recycling his material at every opportunity. 'Tactus eruditus' (the well-informed touch), for example, was a paper he presented at the Intercolonial Medical Congress in Auckland in 1914, just as his book was being published. It was a short presentation on the valuable clinical information that could be gained by palpation and percussion in the physical examination of the patient. Reliance on seeing and hearing could be augmented by touch and smell, in particular. After the congress, the paper was published in the *Australian Medical Journal*, and in a pamphlet.[14]

Springy saw it as a physician's duty to educate the public in ways of improving health: 'The physician's usefulness must extend far beyond the remedial treatment of the sick. It must be more and more recognized that he is a servant of Nature, able to do more preventatively than curatively, and more valuable by his advice than his drugs.'[15] He cited St John Ambulance first aid courses as one such means that should be encouraged for the public: 'For practical familiarisation with the prompt treatment of emergencies (such as haemorrhage, fractures, insensibility, burns and injuries generally), nothing is better than a St John Ambulance course, either as a pupil, or later on, as a lecturer'.[16] He also saw it as a physician's duty to speak out on matters affecting health and wellbeing, and he was a strong advocate for government responsibility in providing and promoting health services. This had already been seen in his public health pronouncements about tuberculosis, but, as war loomed, it was to be tested as never before.

CHAPTER XXXVII.

CONCLUSION.

At the great London meeting of the International Medical Congress 1881, that silver-tongued orator of his time, Sir James Paget, concluded his great Presidential Address with a magical peroration that has been ringing in many ears ever since.

At the much smaller Dunedin meeting of the Intercolonial Medical Congress in 1896, finding none better, I penultimated my own small address on "The Battle of Life" with the same glowing words.

Now, in 1914, at the close of this pioneer Australian Text Book for Students and Practitioners, I still know no professional expression so true, so consoling, so inspiring.

I leave it, therefore, in your remembrance, as guide and guerdon of our life work.

> "We can claim for our calling from amongst all the sciences, the most complete and constant union of those three qualities, which have the greatest charm for pure and active minds, novelty, utility, and charity.
>
> "We can compete with the world, not where wealth is the highest evidence of success, but in the nobler ambition of being counted among the learned and the good, who strive to make the future better and happier than the past."

In the practical performance of this great privilege and duty there are two underlying principles—one intellectual, the other emotional—which I venture to think worthy of special mention. And since Perfection seems to come only through the combination, I bring them together as my closing thought. Thanks to our Classicist, Professor Tucker, I can present them to you in epigrammatic Latin.

The first, intellectual, Hellenist, the easier for modern scientists to conceive, and the more commonly followed, is the one which I placed upon the title page of my first volume, " Know—and Do :"

et scire semper et agere.

The second, emotional, Hebraic, has no place in our modern curricula of study, but is no less valuable, and even more inspiring. You will find it added to the former on the title page of this second volume. It runs, " Love's immortalized by Death."

Amor per mortem immortalis.

Figure 27: Textbook concluding chapter page

Figure 7: Tom Roberts's portrait of Annie

Figure 17: Springthorpe Memorial (a) glass ceiling, (b) the tomb

Figure 18: Mackennal sculptures

Figure 38: Springthorpe Park gates

Figure 39: Springthorpe Boulevard, Macleod

6. Egypt

When war was declared, Springy enlisted straight away, on 19 October 1914.[1] His departure was scheduled for late November. He had a strong sense of loyalty to Australia, and to 'home', as Britain was still thought of by many Australians. Though he was now fifty-nine years of age, there was no doubt in his mind that every able-bodied man should enlist. Indeed, later in the war, when recruitment of replacement troops became difficult and conscription was mooted, he strongly supported the idea. Although the proposal was twice rejected by the Australian population, Springy remained vocal about it. He criticised the able-bodied for not enlisting, and the government for not being forthright enough about their duty to serve. He noted in his diary that Lord Geddes (then Director of National Service in the Lloyd George cabinet) in the *Morning Post* of 17 September 1917 'recalls my plea of March 1916 "Serve—not enlist"'.[2]

Melbourne *Punch* reported an 'Au revoir' gathering held for Dr Springthorpe three days before he left for Egypt:

> An au revoir 'at home' was given to Dr. Springthorpe on 25th November by Miss Rose Paterson of 'Matlock House,' Caulfield, which proved a most enjoyable and representative gathering. The hostess welcomed the guests in the lounge-room, which was prettily decorated with Lady Gray roses and palms, contrasting very effectively with the rose du Barrie carpet and furnishings. The guests arrived at 9 o'clock, and supper was served in the dining-hall where the beauties of the brown-toned furnishings were greatly added to by the decorations, which were in yellow blooms, interspersed with trails of asparagus ferns. The tables were very cleverly arranged in a square, so that all the guests faced each other, and the space in the centre was converted into an island of palms and tall, graceful Japanese bamboo rushes.

The supper was very daintily done. Artistic souvenir cards were placed for each guest, bearing the inscription, 'Au Revoir to Dr. Springthorpe,' over which waved the Union Jack and Australian flag. Drs. Springthorpe and Syme, being the principal guests, were given the seats of honour.

During supper several toasts were given. Dr. MacAdam spoke of the war in general, then said they had met to bid farewell to their old friends who were leaving within a few days for the front. Dr. MacAdam said he had known Drs. Springthorpe and Syme for many years, and to know them was to love them.[3] He thanked their hostess for the privilege of meeting at 'Matlock House,' and trusted before long they would be together on a similar occasion to bid them a welcome home. Dr. Springthorpe who looked well in the uniform, made a very patriotic speech. He spoke feelingly of the friends he was leaving in Australia, and, with a few nicely chosen words to his hostess, called for a toast to the proprietor of 'Matlock House.' Dr. Syme, who is well known for his 'dry humour,' gave a very glowing speech, and trusted they would all meet again in the near future. Miss Rose Paterson, who was called upon for a speech, very gracefully called upon the chairman of directors, Mr. Hardie, who said he would try to be Miss Paterson and on her behalf welcome the guests, and said how pleased she was to see them and thanked the Doctors who spoke so kindly of her and 'Matlock House.' On being called on again to speak, Miss Paterson called upon Master Guy Springthorpe, who, to the surprise of all, made a youthful and happy speech.[4] The evening closed with 'Auld Lang Syne.'[5]

Matlock House was a large mansion (originally named 'Vadlure') situated on a large block of land bounded by Alma, Kooyong and Dandenong Roads in North Caulfield, which had become a private hospital. It was used by patients of Springthorpe and many of the other doctors present at the function. Several of the doctors later joined Springy at war. George Adlington Syme, Springy's contemporary and co-guest of honour, was a senior surgeon at the Melbourne Hospital and, later, founder of the College of Surgeons, serving as its first president.[6]

In November 1914, Enid, aged twenty-five, sailed to England in order to marry a New Zealander, George Knyvett Totton. The wedding took place on 24 April 1915 at Christ Church, Woburn Square, London. As her father was on military service, the bride was given away by her uncle.[7] Totton was a senior executive of the New Zealand Insurance Company.[8] After having managed their branch in Yokohama, Japan, for several years, he was now about to head their branch in Rio de Janeiro. Enid gave birth to a son there, Berners Knyvett Totton, in February 1918.[9] The family subsequently lived in England and had one further son, John Anthony Totton, in 1922.

Springy kept a diary during the war, which he thought might be of use to future historians. Afterwards, he had it typed, with several carbon copies. The main copy he donated in 1926 to the Mitchell Library in Sydney. Another was donated by his widow in 1934, along with many other papers, to the archives of the Australian War Memorial in Canberra, and a third was donated in 1971 by his son, Dr Guy Springthorpe, to the Medical History Museum at the University of Melbourne. Each of the copies is liberally sprinkled with handwritten marginal annotations, all essentially the same, although there are slightly more in the Mitchell Library copy.

Being a senior physician at the Melbourne Hospital, Springy was appointed as a lieutenant-colonel in the Australian Army Medical Corps. Rank was important to him as evidence of his status. Although staff for No. 1 Army General Hospital (AGH) were generally recruited from Melbourne, and staff for No. 2 AGH from Sydney, Springy was reassigned to No. 2, apparently because of slowness in the recruitment of senior doctors in Sydney. He noted that some of No. 2 AGH's staff had antecedent military experience, but that No. 1 AGH staff did not. He also noted that Lieutenant-Colonel Ramsay Smith of Adelaide had been appointed officer commanding No. 1 AGH, and predicted that, due to a history of authoritarian conflict, he was likely to experience difficulties with his staff: 'A good man but "blackleg" in the medical profession—soon at loggerheads'.[10]

In his first diary entry for the war, Springy recalled giving his farewells before setting sail on 28 November 1914:[11] 'Goodbye to "Joyous Gard"—last look around "Camelot"—past instructions—board "Kyarra" about 12—time ordered for 5.45 but crowd kept in ignorance—long wait for wives, sweethearts, mothers, fathers, sisters and friends—Auld Lang Syne—streamers—so off to war'.[12] On board the *Kyarra*, a steamer of 10,200 tons, were No. 1 and No. 2 AGH, the 1st and 2nd Stationary Hospitals, and the 1st Casualty Clearing Station staff: a total of sixty-six medical officers, a hundred and sixty-one nurses, sixty-two sergeants and five hundred and three men. It was the first Australian ship sailing as a medical ship under the Geneva Conventions.[13] The voyage to Alexandria took nine days, with a three-day stopover in Ceylon (now Sri Lanka).

The Australian Imperial Force, when it departed Australia in November 1914, was expecting to go to the war in Europe. However, Turkish affiliation with Germany led to a rapid change in plans. Initially, there was some deployment to protect the Suez Canal, followed soon after by a British High Command decision to carry out an amphibious landing at Gallipoli. This was aimed at opening a second front for the war and securing passage through the Dardanelles. Australian troops were therefore diverted to an encampment in Egypt before the attack on Gallipoli.

The AIF chief of general staff was Major-General Sir William Bridges.[14] Surgeon-General William Williams was director of medical services.[15] However, upon arrival in Egypt, the Australian and New Zealand Army Corps (ANZAC) was formed by combining the two forces under the command of British Major-General W. R. Birdwood, who had been specifically appointed by Lord Kitchener, British Secretary of State for War. Birdwood appointed the British general Richard Ford as director of medical services in Egypt, while Williams was deployed to England. Bridges was subordinate to Birdwood.[16] When the unit arrived in Alexandria, Egypt, on 14 January 1915, it entrained to a camp at Mena, about sixteen kilometres from Cairo, near the Great Pyramids. No. 2 AGH was set up in Mena House, which Springy described as 'a winter sanatorium for millionaires',[17] though the troops were accommodated in tents on flat, sandy ground nearby. The site had been selected by Lieutenant-Colonel Neville Howse, staff officer to Surgeon-General Sir William Williams. Later, it was discovered that the grounds flooded in November each year and had to be abandoned. In the meantime, the hospital was inspected by General Bridges, who declared it 'excellent',[18] and by General Ford.

Figure 28: Mena House, No. 2 AGH.

Figure 29: Mena camp

When the hospital was officially handed over, Springy noted that Howse said he did not want bacteriology or X-ray units. 'He may not, but we do!' – Springy regarded this as an indication that Howse had insufficient regard for the scientific and human aspects of medicine and focused too much on logistics.[19] Howse was a fifty-one-year-old, English-born surgeon who had emigrated to New South Wales in

1889 and volunteered with the second Australian contingent to the Boer War. He was awarded the Victoria Cross for rescuing a wounded soldier under gunfire and ended the war with the rank of honorary major. He remained in the Australian Army Medical Corps Reserve as a major until he volunteered with the expeditionary force to German New Guinea in 1914, when he was promoted to the rank of lieutenant-colonel. From there, he joined Williams's staff.

Within the first two weeks, Springy became alarmed at the number of men being admitted to hospital with pneumonia. He concluded that this was due to overcrowding, insufficient relaxation, and too much marching with heavy packs for prolonged periods without rest. He complained about this and was very pleased when General Birdwood ordered one day's rest each week and better rations. 'Birdwood was always solicitous of his men', commented Springy.[20]

Figure 30: Troops marching in the desert

At the same time, his prediction about No. 1 AGH had come true. There was widespread dissatisfaction in the staff which continued until the director-general of the British Army Medical Services, Sir Alfred Keogh, recommended in August 1915 that the commanding officer, matron and registrar all return to Australia.[21] Springy believed that the root of the problem lay with faulty selection of staff, Smith's lack of military knowledge and an erroneous expectation that an army medical hospital could be run along civilian lines.[22]

However, the high frequency of pneumonia cases continued and was made even worse by dust storms. Springy noted that no officers were affected, that this prevalence was not typical for the Egyptian population, and that it did not occur in other units employing less excessive training regimes. He made further complaints in February 1915, but these were not passed on to higher authorities. Two months later he met General Ford, and spent an hour and a half telling him about the extent of infectious diseases – influenza, measles, gastroenteritis, and pneumonia – 'perpetuated by Bell tents, insufficient breakfast and lunch, overwork from the jump'.[23] He added that 'even the horses had three weeks off!' Springy noted that Ford 'thanked me for the information, agreed with practically everything said, inferred that Howse was to blame, and promised to remove the Light Horse and condemn Mena [dismantle Mena camp]'.[24]

The Light Horse troopers suffered the highest rates of illness and needed better accommodation for their work. The campsite at Mena, as previously noted, was on a floodplain and especially unsuited. But in the end, nothing was done: 'Most say this is because Ford did not remember promises or intentions'.[25] One of Springy's colleagues, the Assistant Director of Medical Services, Mudros (ADSM), speculated that this was because the present heads of Royal Army Medical Corps (RAMC) were the survivors of the early pioneers. They were so old that thirty per cent of them had been designated 'not to be employed again', but despite this, had been employed in the great emergency – 'and ADMS Egypt, ADMS Alexandria *etc* were among these 30%—and ruled us!'[26]

This was the beginning of a long campaign by Springy for Australian medical services to be commanded by Australian senior officers rather than British ones. It also marked a strengthening of his determination to provide the soldiers with more humane treatment. He lamented the authorities' want of consideration for the troops, and their failure to even try to offer any form of recreation or interest at Mena camp. Such recreation would reduce the incentive for visits to Cairo, where the men would 'line up outside brothels and loll about drinking poison'. He believed that the military had the responsibility to care for the mental and physical needs of these young men, rather than just working them 'like machines'.[27]

A few days later, on 11 April, it was announced that the Ghezireh Palace Hotel would be the new location for No. 2 AGH, replacing the Mena House hospital at a cost of £1,500,000. The palace had been built by Khedive Ismail to entertain dignitaries during the opening of the Suez Canal in 1869, after which it became one of the Egyptian royal palaces of the Muhammad Ali dynasty, until it was sold in 1889, becoming a hotel in 1894.

Springy suggested that the adjacent casino should become an annexe for a further two hundred patients, but this was not done. Instead, two other buildings were leased. One was Luna Park, the first Western-style amusement park in the Middle East, which had opened in 1911 and would now serve as an auxiliary hospital for up to twelve hundred convalescing patients. The second was Les Ateliers, a joinery near the hospital. It had a large workroom that was 'filled with palm beds as quickly as they could be procured'. It took up to four hundred patients.[28] Springy was not impressed: 'The Casino was just next door. I would not have held a dog show in Luna Park. Les Ateliers was in sand with a barbed wire fence.'[29]

Figure 31: Three glimpses of the Luna Park hospital annexe

It took a further three weeks for the Ghezireh Hospital to be readied for patients. In the meantime, the ANZAC landings at Gallipoli, starting on 25 April, had resulted in about five hundred casualties arriving to be treated, half at No. 1 AGH and the other half primarily at Mena. Springy condemned the lack of preparation at Ghezireh as 'unpardonable' and predicted that it would be the cause of much subsequent trouble.[30]

In early May, with many of the staff away commissioning Ghezireh, Springy found himself the acting officer in command – for the first and only time in his career – at Mena. He made the most of the opportunity to put his ideas into practice. The following extract from his diary illustrates his close attention to detail, and his interest in every aspect of the patients' lives, not just their medical care:

> Obtained from Matron a list of necessaries for dressings et cetera in each ward—put her on the track of obtaining sufficient cigarettes, papers, cards, games, toothbrushes and other comforts, whilst we are in loco parentis. Notify all that they can cable home at three-quarter rates (cost deducted from pay). Post up eulogistic communications from Cm in Chief, from the King, Admiralty, and Fleet. Take a number of photos to be reproduced at cost price in time for the mail—asked Mrs McN in to give each man a copy of the King's message—send for kits left behind at Alexandria—and arrange x-ray exams at Ghezireh.[31]
>
> Recommend memos from MO's to accompany patients. No case of wound to be discharged without x-ray. No major operation without consultation and report from consulting surgeon to O/C., and no serious or dangerous case to be treated without consultation with the senior surgeon or physician (all new and needed). Obtained 10 shillings per fortnight for each patient from his pay—rearrange hospital, sign many forms for comforts at paymaster's deductions—Matron responsible for papers, donations, et cetera—clear out the lounge and nurses [sic] old sitting-room—bad cases to have best lit and ventilated beds.[32]
>
> A visitor called at irregular intervals, but that was about all—when I took control, I hurried up the YMCA for games

etc., got things through benevolent ladies like Mrs McN. but by establishing the system of the local canteen and payment of the men, got almost all they wanted without any intermediary or delay—hurry up convalescent cases to GH duty. Five cases before Permanent Board—Sisters to report absence from meals—arrange further gifts, donations through Ghezireh—inspect routine business after cleaning up the front of the hospital.[33]

The hallmark of Springy's regime was attention to the psychological as well as the medical needs of each patient. He described the men's high degree of compliance with directives, and their satisfaction with the care that they received. For instance, on 28 May he found in his room a mysterious parcel, which contained a framed photograph of wounded ANZAC men who were being treated at Mena, signed 'with love from us all' from staff and patients. He said that it was one of his most prized possessions.[34]

After his transfer to Ghezireh on 2 June, Springy noted that the patients were 'much more depressed than at Mena'. He put this down in part to protracted strain and physical pain, but also to their being treated strictly according to the rules, with almost no visitors, money, clothes, leave of absence or other comforts.[35]

By mid-1915, a second consignment of Red Cross goods was received at Ghezireh, which included pillows, pyjamas, sheets, towels, face washers, and handkerchiefs. But nobody knew it was arriving, and there was no scheme for its distribution, so few items were given out. General Williams had brought the first consignment of sixteen hundred cases of Red Cross goods from Australia to Egypt, but he had been ordered by General Ford to go to England to supervise the transport of Australian wounded to England and to remain there. Williams delegated the handling of Red Cross supplies to Lieutenant-Colonel James Barrett, registrar of No. 1 AGH.

Barrett (1862–1945) was a specialist ophthalmologist, born and educated in Melbourne before he completed his specialist training in England. On returning to Melbourne, he set up a private practice and undertook university research and lecturing, eventually being elected to the university council in 1901. At the outbreak of war, he became honorary secretary of the Australian Red Cross Society, but in October

1914, he joined the Australian Imperial Force with the rank of major, serving without pay until the following May.[36]

Springy had a very low opinion of Barrett. On several occasions, he pointedly noted that Barrett had been rejected for enlistment in Melbourne but had persuaded authorities to accept him as an honorary ophthalmic surgeon, or, as Springy termed it, 'Major for eye work'.[37] Once in Egypt, Springy said, Barrett ingratiated himself with the officer in command, Colonel Ramsay Smith, and with General Ford. He was appointed registrar of No. 1 AGH, then promoted to lieutenant-colonel, and became a paid member of the armed forces.

Another objection was Barrett's taking credit for work he had not done. According to Springy, 'Of 800 eye cases all but 120 were treated by his understudy, Merlet, yet all were certified to their O/Cs by Barrett as under his treatment. Barrett was away.'[38] When the great English surgeon Sir Frederick Treves visited No. 1 AGH in June 1915, Springy noted bitterly that he was 'carefully piloted through Heliopolis by Ramsay Smith and Barrett (saying) "splendid", "wonderful" and wrote home re the landing arrangements "perfect"—both equally untrue and even scandalous compared to the real facts'.[39]

Springy lamented the general lack of foresight, common-sense, and even humanity at the front. Unless disabled, soldiers were given no consideration. As Springy put it, 'Here, throughout Cairo thousands of young heroes treated just as "wounds and fractures nil"'. A violinist who played for the patients, thereby greatly lifting their spirits, was punished with three days' confinement to barracks for being out without a late pass. Springy said that he 'would not have believed the absence of common kindly feeling and sympathy, if not forced on me from all sides'.[40]

Another example of this neglect was the lack of clothing suitable to the Egyptian climate. General Spans, who was in charge of the training of troops, had fought in India and introduced reforms regarding hours of training, summer clothing, and the like. But commanding officers beneath him often upset his plans. Men fainted when carrying out machine-gun drills and other activities in temperatures of forty degrees Celsius, while clad in thick, tight-fitting tunics, protected from the sun by only thin canvas tents. Even after uniforms made of the lighter 'khaki drill' fabric were made available, soldiers went the one hundred kilometres to Cairo clad in thick winter uniforms.

When questioned by Springy, they revealed that although they had been issued with the lighter uniforms, they were not permitted to wear them into Cairo.[41]

Equally inconsiderate was the failure to supply convalescent patients with clothing other than pyjamas, even when they left the hospital grounds. Their shabby appearance caused a scandal, but in response, the officer in command, rather than providing proper clothes, ordered that the men be kept inside the grounds. Springy described one instance:

> Young man McK., temporarily speechless, motionless, and deprived of intelligence by shellshock, taken for a fortnight to a beautiful garden house by two charming well-wishers—on arriving had only pyjamas and soiled stained tunic and britches from the trenches, with very heavy boots and a forage cap. His hostess was ashamed to let him be seen by any visitors, refused to let him wear the tunic and lent him some of her husband's things until he was sent down by special message a linen hat, a soft khaki shirt, some socks, slippers and a handkerchief—she considered his clothing disgraceful. So our heroes went about in Cairo. I sent a case full to Lady Helen and suggested putting the aides-de-camp in them for a garden party![42]

This is a reference to Lady Helen Munro Ferguson, wife of the governor-general of Australia. She was the patron of and driving force behind the Australian Branch of the British Red Cross Society, having inaugurated its foundation by calling a meeting of interested parties at Government House in Melbourne in 1911. She was no mere figurehead; she was actively involved in its administration, hosting much of the relief supplies work in the ballroom of Government House. Springy's irony would not have been lost on her.

Springy was also troubled that his views on the need for dental and physiotherapy services were not being heeded, despite his experience as Dean of the Dental Faculty at the University of Melbourne and President of the Australasian Massage Association. He knew how important dental services were and noted that No. 2 AGH had only two qualified dentists serving Australian troops in Egypt, supported by dental mechanics. They were constantly busy. Springy had offered at the outset to recruit fifty dental staff, but Lieutenant-Colonel Richard 'Bertie' Fetherston, director-general of medical services, had declined. And when Springy offered the services of some eighty qualified masseurs, Fetherston responded in the same vein. Springy was dismayed, questioning whether dentistry and physiotherapy had 'no place on the establishment ... hence, no place in the war?'[43]

Although he could not budge the military hierarchy, Springy felt that he could do something about the poor distribution of Red Cross comforts to the troops. Having been on Red Cross Victorian council, and by keeping a close eye on the newspapers, he knew that Red Cross had held successful fundraising campaigns and sent a great deal of material to Egypt, but it was not reaching the men who needed it. He was also aware that British Red Cross had been considerably more supportive of its soldiers than had its Australian counterpart. He placed the blame entirely at the feet of Barrett, who was responsible for administering the program, and fired off several letters to this effect to Lady Helen. For instance, on 28 June 1915, he wrote that Barrett:

gathered all stores under his immediate control, acted as if he had been appointed to be the local representative and executive. The responsibility of whatever has occurred is entirely upon his shoulders ... The failure which has occurred in our Red Cross operations is mainly owing to this monopoly by Colonel Barrett.[44]

To emphasise the dire straits of the soldiers, Springy went on: 'Nearer the front the failure has been tragic. [There was an] utter insufficiency of stretchers, dressings and necessary drugs on the beach of Gaba Tepe.' On the troopships evacuating the wounded, there was 'No equipment at all ... [they were] lacking rudimentary necessities to say nothing of comforts. Hundreds [reached] Cairo 4–7 days later with field dressings unchanged through lack of supplies.' In an attempt to appear conciliatory, he acknowledged that Barrett carried a very heavy load of responsibilities, too much for any one man to bear, but although this was an explanation, it was not an excuse: 'This attempt to do too much is practically the only cause of the failure of our branch.'[45]

Lady Helen was alarmed. She sent coded cables through official channels to Barrett, seeking reassurance, and received an immediate response: supplies were being received and distributed, pilferage had been negligible, and the gifts were greatly appreciated. In fact, Barrett sent regular lengthy letters over many subsequent months to Lady

Helen, whose replies indicated an undiminished trust in her man on the ground. She also asked a senior Red Cross official, Mr Adrian Knox, to make recommendations on Red Cross program administration.

Figure 32: (a) Lady Helen Munro Ferguson, (b) Colonel James Barrett, (c) Colonel Neville Howse, (d) Mr Adrian Knox.

Knox was a prominent Sydney barrister and a foundation member of the New South Wales Division of the British Red Cross Society. He went with Norman Brooks to Egypt as Australian Red Cross Commissioner for a variety of important tasks. After the war, he became the second Chief Justice of the High Court of Australia.[46]

Springy was not to be deterred. In a letter sent on 15 July 1915, he continued his complaints about the lack of distribution of Red Cross supplies, making unfavourable comparison with agencies such as the YMCA:

> At Mena we had to seek outside help to obtain cigarettes, razors, handkerchiefs, etc. The Matron never saw a requisition form until I gave her one, and never received any communication from Red Cross and no visits by Col Barrett. The Red Cross provided no outings or amusements, in fact did practically nothing.
>
> The contrast between the local hospital started by the British Red Cross and [our] auxiliary hospitals in the way of environment, food and comforts could scarcely be exaggerated. They are as commendable and satisfactory as ours are unsatisfactory and open to condemnation. So far, no trips on the Nile, no motor rides or the like have been started by the Society, though much needed.[47]

He also continued to criticise the evacuation of wounded soldiers from Gallipoli in July 1915, its lack of planning and preparation, and want of not just comforts but of fundamental necessities on the troopships.[48] In late August, Springy's outrage reached its peak. He alleged that Barrett:

> first usurped control and afterwards kept practically everything in his own hands. The main reason which I gave seems also correct, viz, that he was undertaking so many important duties that it was impossible for him to carry out in a thoroughly satisfactory manner. This has now been found correct by the Military authorities who have relieved him of all military duties leaving only Red Cross work ... his heart has never been in this department of the work, and that difficulties and disabilities are

likely to continue from (a) his apparently irresistible inclination to advertisement, of which illustrations are almost innumerable and (b) his habit of taking credit to himself for what is due to others.[49]

But Barrett's soothing response to Lady Helen reassured her that Springy was a lone dissident, out of step with reality. Despite further letters from Springy, Barrett maintained his stance that everything was going to plan. Nevertheless, Knox took on the responsibility for managing Red Cross affairs, and Barrett resigned from this post.

Back in Melbourne, Lady Helen's complacency was shattered by an avalanche of newspaper reports. 'Red Cross scandal: Disgraceful chaos alleged: Indictment by Dr. Springthorpe: "Nothing is more shocking in the history of this war": No depot near Front' shouted the Melbourne *Herald* on 6 September 1915. The article reported on Springthorpe's advice to Lady Helen, which was supported by Colonel Howse's evidence that the men had not received one article of clothing nor one luxury of food to assist their health and comfort beyond the ordinary rations. It was also supported by the testimony of Archdeacon R. H. Richard of Tasmania, a chaplain of the 3rd Brigade, who said there were 'No Red Cross staff, no comforts, not even necessities'.[50]

Lady Helen was dismayed by this bad publicity. She much preferred Barrett's version and initially rejected the Springthorpe allegations as the views of 'a subordinate officer', not worthy of the same consideration as official reports. Even her husband, Governor-General Sir Ronald Munro Ferguson, referred to them as 'the outpourings of an individual'.[51] But *The Herald* was not placated, and called for an independent enquiry, stating that the complaints should be taken seriously, as 'Dr Springthorpe is held in equally high regard as Dr Barrett'.[52]

A few days later, Barrett was relieved of all official posts in Egypt, and it was announced he would be recalled to Australia.[53] Knox asked that six Australian businessmen be sent to Egypt to manage the handling of goods, and four other persons be despatched to work on an enquiry into the matter.[54]

The Herald weighed in: 'The continued attacks made on Colonel Springthorpe in highest quarters, for his fearless criticism of the Red Cross muddle in Egypt, seem a futile method of reply'.[55] In the meantime, stung by the virulence of criticism, Barrett demanded that his good name be cleared by an official enquiry. A committee was set up, with His Honour J. F. Kershaw, judge of the Cairo Court of Appeal, as its president. Two other members were Colonel C. Manifold and Mr F. T. Rowlatt, governor of the National Bank of Egypt. They met over several weeks in September 1915, but their report was not officially published until January 1916, despite various leakages to the press.[56]

At Barrett's request, the committee sought evidence from Major Stanley Argyle, who had also criticised Barrett in letters to Australia, but Argyle denied having made or circulated such charges.[57] Argyle was a radiologist who shared many of Springy's humanitarian views, but as a student, he had been expelled from the University of Melbourne for criticising authority and was understandably wary of getting into the same kind of trouble again. Nevertheless, he remained Springy's good friend. After the war, he entered the Victorian Parliament, where he became Minister for Health and, later, Chief Secretary and Premier of Victoria.[58]

The committee asked Springy to formulate his charges against Barrett, but he refused, arguing that the enquiry should be into the administration of Australian Red Cross, and that the committee should then decide who was responsible for any maladministration. He objected to his criticisms of Barrett being called 'charges'. The report noted that Springthorpe:

> refused to definitely specify the charges he made against Lieut. Colonel Barrett, except on the general lines that Lieut. Colonel Barrett, as chief executive officer, had shown want of prevision, want of supervision, and had been guilty of bad distribution of personal comforts; and that the chief cause of the faulty administration in these respects was that, owing to the multiplicity of his duties, he had been unable to give the time necessary for the adequate administration of the Red Cross business.[59]

Clearly, the committee was troubled by Springy's request for a review of Red Cross administration, and by his refusal to specify charges against Barrett. After reading the letters and hearing both sides, it drew up its own list of charges, which Springy would have to prove and Barrett would have to answer:

1. General charges fixing responsibility on Lt-Col Barrett.

'(He) gathered all stores under his immediate control, acted as if he had been appointed to be the local representative and executive. The responsibility of whatever has occurred is entirely upon his shoulders' (Letter 28/6/15)

'The failure which has occurred in our Red Cross operations is mainly owing to this monopoly by Colonel Barrett' (Letter 28/6/15)

'This attempt to do too much is practically the only cause of the failure of our branch' (Letter 28/6/15)

'These conditions are quite unworthy of the situation of the needs of the sufferers, and of the efforts and works of Australia.' (Letter 15/8/15)

'I can arrive at no other conclusion but that there has been culpable want of prevision of the supervision and distribution on the part of the Executive Officer, who first usurped control and afterwards kept practically everything in his own hands. The main reason which I gave seems also correct, viz, that he was undertaking so many important duties that it was impossible for him to carry out in a thoroughly satisfactory manner. This has now been found correct by the Military authorities who have relieved him of all military duties leaving only Red Cross work.

It is necessary, however, to add that his heart has never been in this department of the work, and that difficulties and disabilities are likely to continue from (a) his apparently irresistible inclination to advertisement, of which illustrations are almost innumerable and (b) his habit of taking credit to himself for what is due to others.' (Letter 23/8/15)

2. At the front

'Nearer the front the failure has been tragic ... Utter insufficiency of stretchers, dressings and necessary drugs on the beach of Gaba Tepe. (Letter 28/6/15)

'Up to date there has been no depot near the front, and no arrangements for forwarding comforts.' (Letter 15/8/15)

Incredulousness at shortage of provisions (Letter 15/8/15)

3. On evacuation troopships

No equipment at all ... on most of the troopships

...lacking rudimentary necessities to say nothing of comforts. Hundreds reaching Cairo 4–7 days later with field dressings unchanged through lack of supplies (Letter 28/6/15)

Same lack of prevision—preparation and placing of comforts—even of fundamental necessities on the troopships (Letter 13/7/15)

4. In Hospitals

Inadequate delayed distribution of special and urgent articles needed for patients, including hats and clothing other than pyjamas. The Red Cross Society has failed to distribute what was required

... the YMCA has been the almost sole distributor of games of all kinds (Letter 15/7/15)

At Mena, we had to seek outside help to obtain cigarettes, razors, handkerchiefs, etc. The Matron never saw a requisition form until I gave her one, and never received any communication from Red Cross and no visits by Col Barrett. The Red Cross provided no outings or amusements, in fact did practically nothing.

The contrast between the local hospital started by the British Red Cross and (our) auxiliary hospitals in the way of environment, food and comforts could scarcely be exaggerated. They are commendable and satisfactory as ours are unsatisfactory and open to condemnation.

So far, no trips on the Nile, no motor rides or the like have been started by the Society, though much needed. (Letter 15/7/15)

Distribution of Red Cross gifts to hospital patients—The same absence of plan, of requisition and of distribution of individual comforts has continued right on to the past few weeks. But where has been our Australian Red Cross? Its executive officer has been away doing something else. (Letter 23/8/15)

5. Transport to Australia

The same tale of neglect applies to transports to Australia. (Letter 15/8/15)[60]

Many witnesses were interviewed over the course of several weeks. Complex organisational matters were considered, not in any attempt to understand their dysfunction, but to assess whether Barrett was responsible for them. The report's patronising tone admonished Springy for not understanding the difference between the Army Ordnance Department's responsibilities and those of Red Cross, and therefore implied that the complaints were irrelevant. Springy knew the distinction, but his concern was about the failure of the two agencies to coordinate their roles, and his wish was for that failure to be investigated, which it was not. The report did, however, acknowledge that the situation was quite complex:

> The Government Department which supplies, or should supply, the necessities such as medical equipment, is known as the Ordnance Department. The Red Cross Society is not a Government Department, but a benevolent society supported by voluntary subscription. Its organisation, [sic] is therefore quite separate from the Government Ordnance Department; It [sic] is necessary to emphasise the point, which must be clearly kept in mind in order to appreciate the value of Lieut. Colonel Springthorpe's attacks on Lieut. Colonel Barrett in the letters he wrote to the Red Cross Council in Australia.
>
> It is very doubtful whether Lieut. Colonel Springthorpe himself sufficiently appreciated the distinction between Red Cross and Ordnance. He had no experience of military matters before this campaign. As he says himself, 'What I know of military matters I have learnt since December last.' On reading through the letters he sent to Australia it is to be noticed that the greater part of the accusation against Lieut. Colonel Barrett deals with matters for which the Ordnance Department is clearly responsible, and which have nothing whatever to do with Lieut. Colonel Barrett and the Red Cross. If Lieut. Colonel Springthorpe had had the distinction between Ordnance and Red Cross clear in his mind, it is almost incredible that he should, in good faith, have made such attacks on Lieut. Colonel Barrett in his capacity of executive officer of the Red Cross. It seems therefore more charitable to assume that at the time

when he wrote these attacks he did not clearly appreciate or understand the distinction.[61]

In the end, the committee exonerated Barrett of all points.[62] It concluded that most of the charges concerned matters outside Red Cross's responsibility. The commanding officer, through his matrons and sisters, was best placed to know what was required. His first concern, and that of a medical service that was inadequately staffed and equipped 'to meet the enormous rush of wounded' was, quite rightly, essentials such as medical equipment, rather than 'little luxuries such as a comb or a pipe'.[63]

Though ostensibly holding an independent enquiry, the committee demonstrated clearly that it was focused on exonerating Barrett, not on examining the basis of Springy's concerns for the troops. In addition to excusing Barrett from responsibility and highlighting Springy's errors, it was fiercely critical of Springy's failure to confer with Barrett:

> There was a clear duty on Lieut. Colonel Springthorpe to have interviewed Lieut. Colonel Barrett and ascertained the facts. He did not perform that duty. From first to last he never went near Lieut. Colonel Barrett. Had he done so, had he gone and discussed matters with Lieut. Colonel Barrett he would have learnt the distinction between Red Cross and Ordnance; he would have learnt that by applying to his O/C, Colonel Martin, he could have obtained all that he required of Red Cross goods either from the stores or by purchase. He would have learnt that the Australian Hospitals were not Red Cross at all. He could have ascertained the truth of many other matters, and so have avoided making misstatements of fact in his letters. If he had gone to Lieut. Colonel Barrett and frankly discussed the whole question with him, one may at any rate express the opinion that those letters would never have been written to Australia at all.[64]

The committee was equally partisan in blaming Springy for other witnesses' views according with his. For example, in rejecting the concerns of one of the nursing staff, they reported:

It is natural to suppose that she did not know what authority was responsible. Then she met Lieut. Colonel Springthorpe, the author of the letters to the Australian Red Cross Council, and there can be no doubt that thenceforward she viewed Lieut. Colonel Barrett as the 'fons et origo mali' [fountain of all evil], and no further inquiry was necessary. We find her arranging with Lieut. Colonel Springthorpe to send in the 'test' requisition to the Red Cross.[65]

The 'test' was a request for supplies that this nurse had submitted to Red Cross, which had not been filled, revealing that Barrett's assertion of responsiveness was not always correct. This evidence was angrily criticised by the committee as being a 'trap' and therefore unworthy of consideration. They were equally dismissive of submissions by other witnesses who agreed with Springy, finding, for example, that one unnamed woman's allegations were the result of her lack of previous experience of war conditions.[66]

Springy found the enquiry process unpleasant, but shrugged it off, philosophically referring to it as 'Barrett's whitewashing committee'.[67] He went on with his everyday work, little appreciating the very damaging repercussions that the report was to have on his career.

The enquiry ended on 12 November 1915. It was stated that shorthand notes would be available in ten days but, in fact, Springy did not receive them or a copy of the final report for some months. The report was finalised and signed on 4 January 1916. It was forwarded by the Australian High Commissioner in Egypt, Mr A. Henry McMahon, to His Excellency the Governor-General Sir Ronald Munro Ferguson. It was made public several months later.

Lieutenant-Colonel Barrett was in Cairo for the duration of the Red Cross committee of enquiry. On its completion, he was 'invalided to England for two months on the recommendation of a medical board'.[68] This caused some consternation in Australia, where he was previously to return for the final enquiry into the conflict at No. 1 AGH. As registrar at the hospital, he (and officer in command, Lieutenant-Colonel Ramsay Smith) had demeaned and belittled Matron Jane Bell, to the point where her position was untenable. After an official enquiry in Egypt in August 1915, Ramsay Smith and Matron Bell were ordered back to Australia. Barrett, however, remained in Egypt, and now went to England.

A flurry of telegrams sought to clarify the conflicting rulings. In parliament, the Minister for Defence, Senator George Pearce, clarified that regardless of the Bell enquiry, Barrett had been relieved of all military duties and was to return to Australia. Ramsay Smith and Matron Bell were also dismissed from service. Barret subsequently returned to Australia, and his Red Cross work was taken over by Knox's team.[69]

Springy was eligible to return home after a year in service. His official recall was in December 1915, but there was no boat until after Christmas, when two convoys were scheduled to leave. He busied himself with Christmas arrangements for his staff and patients, before he farewelled his companions and sailed from Suez on the SS *Ulysses* on 3 January 1916, landing in Melbourne on 5 February.[70]

During the journey, Springy occupied himself by writing the story of the Gallipoli evacuation. He had read the account by the official historian, Charles E. Bean, and considered it 'quite unworthy'. He submitted his account for censorship and publication permission through official channels and, after approval was granted, he telegraphed it from Fremantle. He pondered the value of his work, even when it was 'one-sided, wrong, and personal', musing that good had come from his extra efforts, even though 'authorities regard me as dangerous, and officious'.[71]

The story, *The great withdrawal—Story of a daring plan—Last days at ANZAC—How our soldiers left*, was published in *The Age* on 1 February 1916. It was a sensation. After giving a harrowing account of the campaign's difficulties and the inevitable conclusion that it was doomed, he described the implementation of the withdrawal plan. It took place without any casualties:

> The only day for eight long months of which such a statement would be true. So, thanks to Providence and to Australian ingenuity, intelligence and discipline, we have retired with honor from an untenable position, and earned the right henceforward and for ever to rely upon ourselves, and to manage our own affairs, subject only to supreme command. The flitting from

Anzac, the most wonderful incident in a wonderful series, is the high-water mark of Australian achievement.[72]

Such rhetoric went a long way towards establishing the anniversary of a major military defeat as our most important national day of commemoration.

Springy's newspaper story greatly increased his already considerable public prominence. Shortly after his return, he used that prominence to encourage military recruitment, giving a public lecture on the ANZACs at St Columb's Church in Hawthorn. The Age reported the next day:

> Every seat in the large building was occupied. The lecture was followed with the keenest interest. The lecturer devoted the first part of his remarks to giving reasons why Australians should enlist for the front, and in doing so he made a very fervent recruiting appeal ... The standing characteristics of our boys in Gallipoli (for they were nearly all boys) were pluck and wonderful endurance and the absence of complaining. No matter what treatment they received, they never complained. Their whole conduct in this respect had filled him with unbounded admiration. Was it not worth while for men to consider whether they should not join a band like this?[73]

Springy submitted his reports of his service in Egypt and England to the Minister for Defence and was interviewed by the Director-General of Army Medical Services. He was initially recorded as having finished his service, but this memo and Gazette notice were recalled, and he accepted the post of senior medical officer on the transport ship *Orsova*, sailing on 16 March 1916 with fifteen hundred men.[74] His eventual deployment would be in the hands of the director of medical services in Egypt.

A marginal note in his diary said: 'Incidentally, at few days' notice get married. Sail next day.' His marriage on 15 March 1916 was to Daisie Evelyn Johnstone, the nurse who worked in his private practice rooms and the daughter of Jessie Johnstone, his long-time housekeeper at 'Joyous Gard'. Springy was now sixty-one, while Daisie was in her mid-thirties.[75] Nineteen years had passed since Annie's tragic death. The event was reported in the social columns:

His bride, Miss Daisy [sic] Evelyn Johnstone, is the youngest daughter of Mrs. J.L. Johnstone, and granddaughter of the late Captain J.E. Moodie, RN., of Hobart. The ceremony was performed in the drawing room of Mr. and Mrs. W.F. Dougall's house, The Burrows, Brook-street, Hawthorne, [sic] by Chaplain-Colonel Nye. Mrs. Springthorpe is at present staying with Mrs. Dougall at their country estate, Mount Franklin. Only a very few intimate friends were present at the wedding. The bride is said by them to have looked charming in an ivory Ottoman silk coat and skirt, and a white panne hat mounted with ospreys. She carried a bouquet of white roses, and was given away by her mother, and attended by her friend, Miss Nell Dougall, as bridesmaid. After April 1 Mrs. Springthorpe will return to Melbourne and there await the return of her man at Camelot, 83 Collins Street.[76]

Springy had become engaged to Daisie during his leave, and when he was recalled to active service, they had decided that their marriage should be expedited.[77] The ceremony followed the rites of the Methodist Church of Australasia.[78] Daisie's mother, Jessie, went to work for the Boyd family.[79]

Upon his return to Egypt, Springy stopped at Suez on 13 April 1916,[80] before disembarking three days later. He reported to Howse, who was now director of medical services. Springy was one of the senior officers who had strongly supported Howse's promotion to this position, reasoning that an Australian would much better serve the interests of Australian troops than did his British predecessors. But it was not long before he regretted his advocacy, coming to the view that Howse failed to stand up for Australian interests against British seniors. In the meantime, having lost his place at No. 2 AGH, Springy was sent as a supernumerary officer to No. 3 AGH, in the Abbassia neighbourhood of Cairo.

The Kershaw report was released to Red Cross and to Springy in January 1916. Miss Philadelphia Robertson, official secretary of the Central Council of the Australian Branch of the British Red Cross Society, gave a report of the council's meeting of 14 March, which mentioned that:

A report of the committee appointed by Sir Henry McMahon, High Commissioner, to enquire into the allegations against Red Cross administration in Egypt, was laid before the council, and much gratification was expressed at the satisfactory nature of its contents. The report was remitted to the Finance Committee.[81]

Springy managed to write a quick response on the day of his departure overseas:

> The statement is incorrect. The committee appointed was in response to a request from the chief executive officer to inquire into charges against himself. The committee declined to enlarge the scope of the inquiry, although informed that what was wanted by Australia was an independent inquiry into actual conditions. This was not held.[82]

In the meantime, the Kershaw report was released to the public. Springy was shocked at the reaction. The exoneration of Barrett was taken by the press to mean that Springy's allegations were unfounded. He protested that in focusing only on Barrett, it failed to address his complaints. This was ignored in a wave of sympathy for Barrett. The *Medical Journal of Australia* subsequently editorialised:

> These gentlemen were eminently suited to weigh the evidence impartially and to arrive at an equitable and fair decision. They have now issued their report.
> Lieutenant-Colonel J.W. Barrett has been completely exonerated. We offer him our sincere congratulations ... The committee has expressed the opinion that Lieutenant-Colonel Barrett had the reputation of being an exceptionally capable man, and that he had been picked out by General Williams because of his capabilities. They have further expressed the opinion that the violence of Lieutenant-Colonel Springthorpe's criticism went far beyond moderation and beyond what the circumstances justified. They consider that Lieutenant Colonel Springthorpe had a solemn duty, which he failed to perform. That duty was to have interviewed Lieutenant-Colonel Barrett, with the object of ascertaining the facts before any charges were made.

These deplorable incidents might have been prevented altogether had everyone serving at the time in Egypt recognized the one object which had impelled men to leave the Commonwealth for the scene of military activity. There appears to be no question whatsoever about the value and wholeheartedness of the services which Lieutenant-Colonel Barrett was rendering to the Empire. We must presume that the trenchant criticisms levelled against him had their origin in the desire to increase the efficiency of the Australian Army Medical Service. They were, however, peculiarly unfortunate in that they created disharmony when harmony was needed and discord when all units of the Empire should have been acting in unison in a great endeavour to achieve one purpose. The incident is now past history, and the Red Cross Society retains the valuable co-operation of Lieutenant-Colonel Barrett.[83]

In response to such newspaper articles reporting the conclusions of the Egyptian enquiry, he wrote a letter saying that no enquiry had been held into the actual shortcomings he had identified, that Mr Knox of Red Cross had declined to make a second investigation of facts, and that all Springy's suggestions for improvements had been adopted: Red Cross had accepted Barrett's resignation and replaced him with administrators who actually did the work that should be done.[84] The letter was not published.[85]

On the introductory pages of his copy of the Kershaw report (which his widow donated to the Australian War Memorial in Canberra), Springy wrote a note repudiating the criticism he received from Red Cross. He felt vindicated, and compared himself to Lieutenant-Colonel R. Markham Carter (1875–1961) of the Indian Medical Service. Carter had come to public attention in 1914 through his revelations of shocking medical conditions in Mesopotamia, such as casualties 'lying inert amid stalactites of faeces'. Carter was initially subjected to stormy interviews in which he was accused of insubordination, with threats to his career. However, after an enquiry he was eventually exonerated and praised as courageous, his revelations leading to a major scandal and the resignation of India's viceroy, secretary of state, and commander-in-chief.[86]

This analogy enabled Springy to stoically endure the serious damage that the Kershaw report had done to his reputation. However, it prevented him from understanding his own contribution to the mess. The puritanical view that when people suffered neglect, someone should be held accountable and punished was a recurring theme in his work. By deciding that blame for all the failings of Red Cross administration fell on Barrett's shoulders, Springy triggered a vendetta that eclipsed any possibility of constructive problem-solving. Sadly, he did not learn from this experience, and was doomed to repeat it.

However, Philadelphia Robertson's comments accurately reflected the views of the Red Cross establishment and the written records in its archives. The 2014 centenary history of Australian Red Cross went further. Far from seeing Springy's complaints as a means of resolving implementation difficulties, it recriminated: 'In an action designed to humiliate Lady Helen and tarnish the reputation of Australian Red Cross, Springthorpe's complaints were leaked to the Australian press.'[87] It went on to describe Lady Helen's reaction:

> In the meantime, she went on the offensive. Any whiff of scandal could damage the momentum of the fledgling organisation in Australia and threaten her authority. 'I feel deeply for those who, having worked so hard, and sacrificed so much, are being depressed by these charges of failure in Egypt,' Lady Helen declared in the press. 'I feel it necessary to grasp some of those nettles which have sprung up in the path of the Red Cross Society.' She argued that these 'nettles' had their origin in a misunderstanding: Colonel Springthorpe did not grasp the society's true aims, the limitations it faced, or the conditions in which it had been working—particularly the chaos of those critical first weeks of the Gallipoli campaign.[88]

The findings of the Kershaw committee were described and interpreted as a vindication of Red Cross work:

> This brought to a close a bruising experience for Australian Red Cross, its first highly publicised internal stoush. Although the crisis had little long-term impact on the reputation of Red Cross in Australia, it revealed that better management was required both at home and abroad.[89]

In essence, this was the practical result that Springy had been seeking, but his sanctimonious method had, indeed, resulted in his being treated as a whistle-blower. However, he was not vindicated like Major Carter and the incident remains a lasting stain on his reputation.

Springy spent four months in Abbassia, mainly assessing troops for return to Australia. During this time, he suffered from some health problems. He was admitted to hospital on 3 June for mild fibrositis (a term then used for low back pain). Then, from 20 June, he was admitted to hospital four times for pyelitis (urinary tract infection affecting the kidneys), until he was finally declared unfit for service on 13 August and sent to England for further treatment.[90]

7. England

Springy embarked from Alexandria aboard the *Kanowna* on 13 August. On arrival, he was admitted to the 1st London General Hospital for a couple of weeks, before he was allowed out for convalescence, then finally discharged on 14 September.[1] It was determined that he would not return to Egypt but would remain for service in England. After being interviewed by senior officers at the Australian Army Headquarters in Horseferry Road, he was granted four weeks' leave. Then, he would begin his new role.

During his time in London, Springy stayed with his sister near Russell Square. In his usual energetic style, he was there for only three days before he set off on 4 September for a ten-day visit to Scotland and the north of England. On his return, he spent the next fortnight in and around London. After reporting to the director of medical services on the appointed date, he was told to report to No. 3 AGH at Brighton on 5 October, effectively giving him a further few days' leave.

Springy used the time to visit a variety of places, first calling on fellow Melburnian Major General John Monash, commander of the new 3rd Division. They met at Salisbury Plain, where Springy witnessed a review of troops by King George V. He was introduced to Lieutenant-General Keogh, Director-General of the British Army Medical Services, by whom he was cordially received.

Figure 33: King George V and General Monash reviewing troops

Two days later, on 2 October, Springy visited the Maudsley Hospital in Denmark Hill, then designated the 4th London General Hospital. The hospital was designated 'for neurological cases', a euphemism for psychiatric disorders that the British Army liked to pretend did not exist. He was taken around by the consultant in charge, Dr Mott, and was keen to hear his views about treatment. Springy was, however, a little dismayed by the large number of patients. The hospital held one hundred and sixty beds, which he felt were too many – 'Good for records and medical officer experience but bad for patients'.[2]

The next day, he went to the orthopaedic hospital at Shepherd's Bush, whose staff were expert in two areas of his interest, massage (physiotherapy) and electrical therapy (myotherapy). This pleased him greatly, as he felt it vindicated his advocacy for physiotherapy, which had been disregarded by his own authorities. The next morning, he visited rheumatic and rheumatoid cases at Mile End, East London, and in the afternoon went to see cardiac cases at Hampstead under Sir William Osler, Sir Clifford Allbutt and Sir James McKenzie. Springy was impressed by the introduction of new diagnosis and treatment by testing not what the cardiac waves were saying, but what the heart muscles were doing.[3]

On 11 October, Springy received a letter from the director of medical services, re-assigning him to 3rd Army Auxiliary Hospital Dartford. He reported on that same afternoon to the hospital's commanding officer, Lieutenant-Colonel Henry Powell, who asked him to 'organise [an] electrical massage and orthopaedic department'. Although slightly puzzled as to why he had been reassigned, Springy nevertheless found Dartford to be 'a fine hospital—splendidly equipped and furnished', and found Powell very supportive of his work.[4] He began on 18 October, immediately arranging for his staff to visit other hospitals whose methods he wished to implement at Dartford and setting up protocols for treatment regimens applying those methods. Integral to his regime were complete case histories and records of treatments and responses. His diary note on 30 October proved prophetic of his later battles with the Repatriation Department back in Australia:

> Still organising—first morning taking histories (complete family, personal, war source, disabilities, dates, and symptoms from first to last, giving different hospitals then present examinations as per scheme in my text book for the Melbourne Hospital records.) (I do not think any other records in the AIF are so complete. Fancy if all were similar. Instead of the few scattered notes one usually sees). (And yet these are 'all the pertinent facts and the basis of future pensions. In innumerable cases, injustice has then been done.)[5]

Figure 34: Dartford Hospital ward at Christmas

Under Springy's command, much of the physical treatment was implemented for psychological reasons. The 'graduated exercises' that he prescribed for his cardiac patients suffering palpitations and extreme anxiousness about impending 'heart attack' were as much to reassure them as to strengthen them. As with aphonic cases who became able to speak again, he sought 'sudden replacement of dominant "can't" by a dominant "can".'[6]

Always, the wellbeing of his patients was at the forefront of his thoughts. As Christmas approached, there was a flurry of festive activity in his wards. Whenever possible, he sent patients out on leave, often bending the rules, all the while protesting injustices:

> Some 40 of mine off on furlough—as only one furlough a man—give sick leave instead, regarding both as therapeutic procedures and trusting the men, explaining, advising and examining on his return. Have not had a case requiring censure, except one (Murphy, amnestic—too risky). The more I see of the regulational treatment of the men, the less it seems just, necessary or advisable—it is shocking to men who have volunteered and given up so much if not all. And the cruel unnecessary differences made between Officers and men, justifiable only if they were a different and superior class of being and as if the men did not deserve and could not be trusted. The result is they are denied justice, treated inconsiderately, harshly and unfairly and so are apt to return badness for injustice and go to the devil. The cruelty, the irreparable loss of it and the calm careless injurious way in which they are boarded, the disability often only half stated, at times and not stated all, e.g. one 'gastritis' yes, but also 'shellshock 12 months' no, knowing nil for a week, no memory of home, sent back to the Front; another shellshock and burial without a note on his Board paper.[7]

Complaints filtering back about deplorable conditions for patients boarded at a hospital in Weymouth, waiting for return to Australia, prompted Springy to make a visit to see for himself. Together with Colonel Murdoch, a representative of Red Cross, their visit was able to arrange for important changes, highlighted in his critical report:

Report

1. Men waiting for hours in wet and cold for transport to hospital— new arrangements
2. Huts cold—men sleeping in clothes—(fresh blanket—special cases in better quarters)
3. Waiting for examination in exposed cold—to cease
4. Classifications—hurried and insufficient examination—more searching and undercover
5. Special cases—more facilities and special treatment
6. Continuity of treatment—to be started by recommendations from us
7. Exercise with motive, interest, utility as at Roehampton, et cetera
8. Utilisation of convalescence—as at Shepherds Bush, et cetera
9. Sick leave as a therapeutic procedure—to be arranged under Mrs Spencer Brown and committee
10. Red Cross to make the huts less dreary and more comfortable—add library, silence room, etc—arranged by Murdoch
11. Thus, we can now send on our cases with confidence. (Yes—but why not all foreseen and done from HQ?).[8]

On the same day that Springy sent in his report, 25 January 1917, the announcement was received that the director of medical services, Neville Howse, had been awarded the KCB (Knight Commander of the Order of Bath). Springy had long been disappointed with Howse and complained in the privacy of his diary about Howse's perceived lack of care for hospitals, failure to stand up for Australian interests against the British, and lack of planning and strategy. According to Springy, his patients often waited about for months for proper treatment or relocation, with others being sent back to the front, to their detriment. Springy also lamented Howse's failure to obtain ships for transporting unwell soldiers out of the war zone.[9]

On 29 June, Springy submitted a request to Army command to visit hospitals dealing with shellshock cases, located behind the firing lines in France. He wished to see whether his ideas about treatment were practicable under front line conditions, but his request was refused weeks later with a curt 'Not approved'.[10] He wrote to Howse seeking an explanation but did not receive one. This added to his impression of Howse as a person who did not have the backbone to argue with authorities on behalf of his men's interests.

This impression was intensified a few weeks later when Springy heard that Howse wanted men with shellshock to be sent to Weymouth. In Springy's opinion, this was 'unpardonable ignorance or callousness', because the auxiliary hospital at Weymouth was only a staging post for patients' return to Australia.[11] There was considerable pressure on medical staff in all the army general hospitals to move patients on, preferably back to the battlefield, but, failing that, to Weymouth and home. Weymouth accommodated up to four thousand patients, served by only seven medical officers. Treatment for physical injuries was minimal, with virtually none for psychological trauma.[12] The waiting time for transport back to Australia depended on available shipping and could be as long as several months. For shellshock patients, this would mean no treatment until they arrived back in Australia – and in many cases, not even then – a plan directly contrary to Springy's views about early and sustained treatment.

Springy objected to the frequently premature termination of treatment and generally poor conditions. The main reason, he thought, was that the Australian Army Medical Service had no dedicated hospitals in England that could properly appraise a patient's treatment needs before deciding where to send him, so Australian patients ended up scattered between hundreds of English hospitals, which were keen to repatriate them. He blamed Howse for failing to stand up for Australian hospital allocation equivalent to that achieved by Canada.[13]

In July 1917, Springy's commanding officer, Colonel Powell, who had supported Springy's methods, was promoted and sent to command a hospital in France. His replacement, Lieutenant-Colonel B. Milne Sutherland, was given his orders by Howse: 'clear out 1000 a week—keep nothing beyond a few weeks, and only those if absolutely necessary'. Springy was clear that Howse's ultimatum was 'if he cannot, he goes'.[14]

In contrast to his views on Howse, Springy's opinion of Sir Alfred Keogh, director-general of the British Army Medical Services, was favourable. Keogh was a 'splendid head', who believed that the role of Red Cross was 'to do what Red Tape prevented the army from doing'; as Springy wrote, 'that was always my view and it was in accord with therewith that I acted in Egypt'.[15] This rekindled Springy's feelings of injustice at his treatment by the Egyptian enquiry. He saw himself as a whistle-blower whose views would ultimately be vindicated, and again compared his pillorying to that meted out to Markham Carter of the Indian Medical Service. The main difference, as Springy saw it, was that he remained vilified, whereas Carter was eventually exonerated.[16] In making this comparison, Springy was drawing a rather long bow.

Over the next few months, Springy accumulated data and opinions about the hospital caseload. Looking back from our current understanding of illnesses, it is hard to imagine the difficulties of assessing disorders within the conventional wisdom of that period. The hundred years leading up to Springy's time had seen a revolution in scientific medicine. The germ theory of disease – along with developments in bacteriology, pathology, pharmaceutics, anaesthesia, aseptic surgery, and, above all, the philosophy of scientific evaluation of practices – had transformed medicine from a craft to a scientific profession. Rejecting old-fashioned remedies and keeping up with the latest discoveries was a matter of professional pride. Springy wanted to be at the forefront of making his field of mental disorders equally scientific as other fields of medicine. However, he faced two major obstacles. One was the difficulty of obtaining measurable data. The other was the stigma surrounding mental disorders.

This stigma has been with us since antiquity. Fears of witchcraft may have faded, but the rejection of someone who is 'not like us' persists to this day. Amid the turmoil of world war, it ranged from contempt for weakness ('pull yourself together') to accusations of malingering and cowardice ('desertion from battle is punishable by death'), with only marginal tolerance of symptoms. The contempt showered on the patients was also suffered to some degree by the doctors who cared for them.

Springy struggled to reconcile his views with those of others working in the field, in order to arrive at a reliable system of classifying mental disorders. Major psychotic conditions like schizophrenia, mania and melancholia were widely recognised, but less disruptive psychological states had no generally accepted diagnostic lexicon.

The contributions of Sigmund Freud added some diagnostic terms and concepts to the discourse, but widely divergent schemata were used in different countries. It was not until after World War II that the World Health Organisation introduced the International Classification of Diseases (including mental disorders) and the American Psychiatric Association introduced its Diagnostic and Statistical Manual of Mental Disorders to give more reliable schemata.

Springy's most immediate problems were of patients with palpitations thought to be 'cardiac cases' (nowadays classified as anxiety disorders), patients with loss of functions such as paralysis, blindness and loss of speech (nowadays classified as hysterical conversion symptoms), and shellshock (nowadays classified as post-traumatic stress disorder). His own view had consistently been that shellshock was 'emotional rather than commotional'. By this, he meant it was a psychological response to events and not an organic physical illness, as had at first been theorised by Dr Mott at Maudsley Hospital. Mott's initial view was that exploding artillery shells caused petechial haemorrhages (small-scale bleeding and bruising) on the surface of the brain. This made the diagnosis acceptable to military authorities, whereas the psychological explanation was not welcome. However, Springy noted that Mott had subsequently accepted the psychological cause.[17]

By September, Springy had accumulated case records and statistics of some three hundred shellshock cases and two hundred cardiac cases. He continued to lobby unsuccessfully for permission to go to France to observe frontline treatment, and grew increasingly disillusioned about the downgrading of his hospital from a place of treatment to a transient waystation for return to Australia. Deciding that his skills might be better used in helping repatriated soldiers, he cabled Australia, offering to return home to organise a treatment program there, but received no reply.

Colleagues confirmed Springy's suspicion that the frontline response to shellshock cases was poor. There were so many cases that the available medical officers had inadequate time to make accurate diagnoses, even if they had the skill to do so. They were not permitted to send shellshocked soldiers to special hospitals, except as 'NYDN' (not yet diagnosed nervously). At these special hospitals, such patients would be diagnosed by experts as either 'shellshock sick', 'shellshock wounded', or 'otherwise'. Patients designated 'shellshock wounded' had bodily injuries, whereas the 'shellshock sick' had no visible injuries, and the 'otherwise' included patients with bodily symptoms such as blindness or paralysis without signs of injury. The significance of this was that only the wounded, and not the sick, were eligible for a gold stripe (sewn on the left uniform sleeve of soldiers who had been wounded in battle).[18]

Springy regarded this as 'strange discrimination', and observed that the presence of a physical wound or concussion often minimised, or even prevented, the emotional phases of 'true' shellshock. For some time, the 'shellshock sick' without wounds were considered malingerers: 'Wandering away out of mind and control, some were even shot for desertion, but never by us'.[19] Indeed, General Haigh, in charge of British troops on the Western Front, requested authority to deal with such cases among the Australians by court martial, with the possible penalty of death by firing squad. Springy strongly opposed this in his interviews with press correspondents and in communications with the Australian Prime Minister, Billy Hughes. The authority was not granted.

At long last, after further lobbying, Springy was granted permission to go to France. He spent the first two weeks of November 1917 on a very busy itinerary, with his observations confirming much of what he had suspected. A high proportion of shellshock cases were being returned to the front despite receiving minimal treatment, and much of the available treatment was provided by staff who had no particular expertise in the field. On his return to Dartford, Springy had a long discussion with Howse about his observations. He noted that Howse wished to return to Australia to oversee the administration of pensions to veterans and their families.[20] This would be important after-war work, as more than twenty-three thousand men had already been repatriated in 1916 alone. Shellshock cases would be among the more difficult ones to deal with, and Howse wanted expert assistance. All of a sudden, Springy became useful to Howse, and his opinions began to matter.

Springy saw himself as an advocate for the men against a bureaucracy that wanted to minimise the number of pensions. He was very aware that the patients' medical records were frequently pitifully inadequate for proving a soldier's eligibility for financial support. He spent much of his time 'fixing up papers'. In his diary, he recorded examples of the gratitude that he received for his empathy: 'as if parting with something personal they give me photos, cigarettes, etc. An Aboriginal says they'll come hundreds of miles to see me.'[21]

With Howse's consent, Springy drew up a 'Shellshock Card' to systematise the recording of case reports. He submitted it to headquarters, but acknowledged resistance by the men because of stigma, and by medical officers because of the additional work. He noted in his diary that it 'was never used until Millard was using it—after the Armistice', and that it was 'only good for the men, not for Headquarters'. This was because medical records generally ignored psychological symptoms, yet those records were the basis for service pensions. At this stage, Colonel Reginald Millard, Australia's assistant director of medical services, who had no experience with mental disorders but was responsible for medical records, needed specialist advice. Although Springy's plan gave men a better chance of receiving a pension, it was not an image of military service that the army wished to convey to government.[22]

(Back of card.)

NEURASTHENIC, HYSTERIC, AND SHELL SHOCK CARD.

Strike out each item that is not applicable.

Name of Patient................Rank............Unit............Reg. No..........

In the family there has been	**Hysteria — Epilepsy — Insanity — Neurasthenia — Nervous breakdown — Nervous instability**
Prior to enlistment patient ...	was: **Highly strung — Alcoholic** had: **Nervous breakdown — Fits — Injury to skull — Syphilis — Insanity — Sunstroke**
The patient himself had/<u>not</u>	become: **Nervy under strain of service**
On............................... At...............................	He had: **Neurasthenia — Hysteria — Shell shock with Wound — Burial — Gas — Concussion**
As a result he became ...	**Dazed — Unconscious — Maniacal — Dumb — Deaf — Stammering — Blind — Amnestic** Had: **Tremors — Headaches** (*frontal : occipital*) **Insomnia — Bad dreams — Vertigo — " Turns "**
He still has	**Head-ache — Confused — Dull — Tremors — Vertigo — Bad dreams — Insomnia — Defective Memory — Power of Concentration — Sight — Hearing — Bad dreams — Insomnia — Defective Memory — Power of Concentration — Sight — Hearing — Stammering — Sweats — Flushes — Palpitations — Gastric — Respiratory — Locomotive troubles — " Turns "** Is: **Dumb — Neurasthenic — Hysterical**
He has developed	**Neurasthenia — Hysteria — Myoclonic spasms — Delusions — Epilepsy — Petit Mal — Mental Wasting**
Other special points noted are	**Hyper-thyroidism — Hyper-Adrenalism — Defensive Reflex acts** (*jumps, flinches, etc.*)

Signed as true and correct.

Signature........ ....

Place.................... Date................ Rank....................

Figure 35: Springy's diagnostic card

As Christmas 1917 approached, Springy slowed down his repatriation of patients and threw himself into festivities. The wards were decorated, Christmas cards were distributed – along with presents provided by Red Cross – and special efforts were made with dining and entertainment. Springy dined with the 'boys' and took part in the speeches and carol-singing. After Christmas, however, the backlog of patients had to be dealt with, and there was enormous pressure to move patients on to Weymouth and home.

Shortly before Christmas, Springy had written to his friend General Monash, describing some examples of inconsiderate management of patients and complaining of inflexibility and lack of common sense among those in command. On 16 January 1918, he received a reply from Monash, 'showing the difficulty of the problem and how anxious the best are to do their best'. He admired Monash's:

> whole and continuous efforts directed day and night to an attempt to eliminate, as far as possible, the evil consequences of inexperience, want of knowledge, want of tact, and want of qualities of leadership in hundreds of individuals in positions of subordinate command and responsibility—impossible to achieve through lecturing and preaching—can only lay down broad principles, watch carefully, deal drastically with glaring ineptitude. That's a man.[23]

He contrasted Monash with Howse, who he believed lacked sufficient scientific knowledge and made no attempt to manage hospitals with the rigour that Monash applied: 'hence Monash's success and Howse's failure'.[24] Springy's disdain for Howse was further bolstered by what he saw as self-aggrandisement. He commented on the fact that after receiving the award of Knight Commander of the Order of the Bath (KCB), Howse had the authority to grant the honour of Knight Commander of the Order of St Michael and St George (KCMG), and gave it to himself.[25] Nevertheless, he continued to deal with Howse appropriately and professionally.

The first few months of 1918 saw heavy fighting on the Western Front. Springy was appalled at the carnage and wanted to go to France to work in the hospitals there, but Howse would not permit it: 'He said I was more useful where I was'.[26] Having turned sixty-two in August

1917, Springy was eligible for retirement, and his family had written, urging him to return to Australia. He wrote home, explaining why he remained:

> Satan and the Almighty contending for all that makes Life worth living, etc—that's why I am here—doing my little bit of infinite importance to some hundreds who have been in or will see Hell before they become unconscious, dream terrible dreams, lose memory and powers of mind—if I don't, no one will. In some cases at least, paying a price, a heavy one, but fading into nothingness compared with that of the 43,000 who will never return—in a crisis such as the world has never seen before—and the end—the overthrow of the wrong—but at such a cost![27]

In February 1918, Springy resigned as a Member of the Royal College of Physicians, insulted that his nomination as a Fellow had been ignored. He had been proposed by two British medical luminaries: the Oxford Regius Professor of Medicine, Sir William Osler, and the Cambridge Regius Professor of Medicine, Sir Clifford Allbutt. Osler appealed for the College to reconsider, but nothing came of it.[28]

Around this time, Daisie suffered a very serious illness, and recuperated in rented rooms in South Yarra, cared for by her mother. Guy and Lance were also with her.[29]

Hearing of a conference on the aftercare of disabled soldiers to be held in London in May, Springy successfully solicited for official Australian representation, and he and Howse attended. Springy presented a paper titled 'Suggestions as to the better treatment of our war neuroses', which was subsequently published in the conference transactions.[30] General Fetherston, director-general of medical services, visited Dartford on 10 May and asked Springy for a report on the work described in his paper. Springy admired Fetherston's energy and determination, noting that he 'goes everywhere, sees everything … different in toto from Howse'.[31]

In Springy's opinion, Canada and New Zealand's services were both better run than Australia's. He lamented that Australia's exhibition at the conference was 'a disgrace', that he made the sole Australian contribution, and that, as a result, 'others must think us mere fighters, not men of plans, views of any depth or breadth ... none of our HQ would have known or cared or gone but for me! (Nice predicament!)'[32]

On 20 May 1918, Springy received from the secretary of the Melbourne Hospital a letter terminating his appointment as physician, a position he had held since 1884 – for some thirty-four years. There was no alternative, because the retiring age was set in the hospital by-laws. He was disappointed, but philosophical: 'so, like all others, out I go, thankful for the opportunity and all it has meant'.[33]

By mid-year, Springy's criticisms of the treatment of soldiers had become more strident. He knew this made him unpopular with his seniors, and speculated: 'I suppose I shall be still more *persona non grata* after being *persona incognita*. What matter, if good follows!' He was particularly incensed that, as a specialist in the field, his conclusions about a soldier's shellshock could be overruled by headquarters staff, simply because the admission doctor's diagnosis had precedence over his. He knew full well that on return to Australia, these soldiers would be denied medical support, their disabilities deemed 'not due to war service' on the basis of faulty diagnoses. He submitted a lengthy report to Fetherston, which proposed making headquarters more 'scientific'; establishing two general hospitals in England to which Australian patients could be sent directly; remodelling the relationship between auxiliaries, convalescents and camps; attending to the men's 'psychology'; using exercise, remedial gymnastics, and occupational therapy; and organising recreation and education. He 'gently suggested' that the other Dominions were doing more along these lines than Australia was.[34]

Far from implementing a therapeutic approach, Australia's aim was to ship as many wounded men home as quickly as possible. The hospital would receive commands to despatch six hundred men a week. Springy's diary showed his ambivalence about senior officer appointments:

> men simply numbers, the staff simply classifying clerks, our service reduced to simply an arithmetical addition sum—and the O/C obeys his instructions and hustles his staff! ... Have HQ been reprimanded? Per contra—all decorated.[35]
>
> ...
>
> Is position any criterion of merit? The war says, 'No'. Is

recognition worth anything? Not even its face value. Is life a just equation? Not this side death—what is the summary? Just my old motto 'et seix semper et agere'—Thank heaven it has been my lot to 'ever try to know and do'—amongst the many and the lowly placed so that there has been no inducement to play for self—There are lesser times when I feel envious and sorry I am not in a higher and wider sphere and wielding wider if not less personal influence—But in my better moods I forget them all and feel more than ever that they are not worth considering.[36]

He showed similar mixed feelings about honours, scorning those who received them for (in his opinion) undeserved reasons, but at the same time, he was bemused that he was unrecognised. At another level, however, he realised that his constant stream of criticisms made him unpopular. He was apprehensive about being 'Stellenbosched': sent to an obscure posting or back to Australia. (Nevertheless, on 28 August 1919, a War Office communiqué was brought to the British Secretary of State for War, reporting on Springthorpe's 'valuable services rendered in connection with the war'.[37]) His research work on behalf of injured soldiers was a consolation too:

I have had my opportunities minimised, but still I have careful full histories of nearly 1000 cases of the best lines, and further than ever I had [at] the Melbourne Hospital. This is my reply and hope— my justification. I have preferred to work to revolt—earlier I would have combined the two. Have I been right? Who knows. It has certainly not been from fear.[38]

Springy spent the last few months of the war sending medical cases back to Australia, before he sailed from Liverpool on board the *Nestor* on 12 December 1918:[39] 'So, farewell England and the war'.[40]

On the ship's arrival in Australia, however, fears of the 'Spanish' influenza pandemic caused great difficulties. Inadvertently, someone had reported a simple feverish cold as 'influenza', so the ship was quarantined at Albany in Western Australia and again at Portsea in Victoria. The soldiers were keen to get home, but tolerated the initial quarantine fairly well, though there was considerable anger at the second. (While Springy was en route, his son Guy fell ill with influenza, but by early February was recovering.[41]) The soldiers were then transported to Broadmeadows Camp, north-west of Melbourne. Springy and other Melbourne residents were released promptly, whereas soldiers from other places had to wait for a further period before discharge, causing huge resentment and some rumblings of mutiny. Springy wrote a letter to Headquarters protesting the unnecessarily restrictive treatment of the soldiers.

Springy noted in his diary that his appointment in the Australian Imperial Force officially ended on 17 January 1919. Nevertheless, his work with the army continued. Such was his notoriety at military headquarters that he was officially called on to explain his public support of the soldiers' discontent and his articles in *The Age* newspaper. He successfully defended himself on the grounds that he had prevented a riot by his support, and that the newspaper articles had been authorised by General Monash.

Springy's private practice had been significantly depleted by his absence. His expenses had continued, but his meagre military income was insufficient to cover them. He calculated that he had made significant losses because of the war, and his future income was now under threat because of the terminations of his university and hospital appointments, both notionally on the grounds of statutory retirement age. Now, he could no longer afford to be philosophical about these redundancies and wished to appeal against them. There was legislation prohibiting dismissal of employees because of absence due to war service, and he hoped this might apply to him as well.

Springy was unsuccessful, both at the hospital and the university. *The Age* reported that, at the relevant meeting of the University of Melbourne council, 'A roar of laughter greeted the reading of Springthorpe's letter, and no action was taken'.[42] But he did resume his work as an official visitor to mental hospitals, and continued his military medical work with returned veterans.

8. Home Again

Springy had been deeply affected by the war. Although he continued to support Australia's involvement in the conflict, he remained bitter about the British sidelining of Australian contributions, and the failure of Australian authorities to stand up to the British. He was also saddened by what he saw as a mindless and heartless bureaucracy. Even as he began to reconstruct his professional life, he continued to battle on behalf of the veterans.

He published a paper on war neuroses in the *Medical Journal of Australia* of October 1919, setting out his classification of mental disturbances and the treatments he saw as appropriate.[1] He estimated that about fifteen per cent of war veterans experienced war neuroses of various types. His recommended treatments were variously based on therapeutic suggestion, re-education, psychoanalysis, physiotherapy, occupation and satisfaction with management.

Springy contrasted the slow, difficult response of psychasthenic and shellshock patients with the rapid response to suggestion shown by patients whom he diagnosed as 'hysterics'. He felt that it was essential to choose the right approach for each patient, lest the treatment become prolonged. Cases with cardiac symptoms but no evidence of heart disease should be given a graduated exercise program and a re-education, aimed at increasing confidence and 'nervous control'. He noted that more than three thousand patients had been successfully treated this way:

> The soldier's psychology, both in health and in disease, has been the outstanding medical feature of the war. Though naturally the incidence is less concentrated and the manifestations less startling in civil life, the factor is still there and, in view of its hitherto general neglect, calls for little less than a revolution in our general principles of practice.

Henceforward, no up-to-date medical school can leave psychology, any more than physiology, out of its curriculum, no teaching hospital can remain without its psychological department, and no up-to-date medical practitioner can leave this priceless talent buried in the dust of ignorance and fight his battle against disease with this, his right arm, tied behind his back.[2]

After his demobilisation, Springy was appointed by the new director-general of medical services, Colonel George Cuscaden, to take charge of neurological and cardiac cases at No. 16 Army General Hospital Macleod (fourteen kilometres north-east of central Melbourne). After four months of work, he reported to Cuscaden on the hospital's conditions and requirements. He also advocated for aftercare treatment and handling of disabled veterans by delivering a series of lectures at Macleod. He illustrated these with photographs produced for English post-war rehabilitation services. As a result, the Minister for Repatriation asked Springy to assist in his publicity campaign and helped his publicity officer arrange a similar series of lectures for Springy.[3]

In February, also with Cuscaden's permission, Springy set up an outpatient clinic for neurological cases at the base hospital. This was intended to help veterans who were receiving pensions but were under no supervision, others who still required expert advice but were not receiving it, and those who were being discharged from military hospital without follow-up arrangements. He sent to the Repatriation Department a report with suggestions as to how they should improve those follow-up arrangements.[4]

Springy published several more papers, including 'Some notes on medical psychology',[5] 'After-care of disabled soldiers',[6] 'Suggestions as to the better treatment of our war neuroses',[7] and 'Some lessons from the war'.[8] In his writings and advocacy, his two main themes were the need to recognise and treat the chronic but unacknowledged psychological problems of veterans, and the need to change the system to avoid such problems occurring in the future. To bring about the latter, in September 1920, he wrote a stinging letter to George Pearce, Minister for Defence (whose responsibilities included the Repatriation Department), about the serious shortcomings of the Army Medical

Service. He requested an official enquiry into these shortcomings and enclosed a copy of his paper 'Some lessons of the war'.[9]

Springy took Pearce's initial thanks and reassurance that the matters would be considered as meaning that an enquiry would be held. When no public enquiry eventuated, Springy's follow-up letter querying when this would occur was quickly labelled by the minister as 'a misconception'. Pearce was to be advised by his own group of military and health consultants. Springy protested, but to no avail. The military bureaucrats closed ranks and informed him that he was not the only doctor with expertise in military matters. Reluctantly, he acknowledged this in his final letter to Pearce:

> I presume it spells finality, but I scarcely like to regard it as such. You are fully aware how serious and widespread were our medical defects during the war. 'No intention of enquiring' is an easy course to pursue. But—does it meet the situation as it should be met? Many of our 60,000 dead and 200,000 casualties call for something very different.
>
> For lesser reasons, perhaps, silence might be kept, if our authorities had learnt the lessons, or if we had some guarantee that 'never again' would the said mistakes recur. But it is futile to expect these from a bureaucratic committee with a bureaucratically limited objective. All precedent is against it.
>
> After such committee has made its recommendations you grant the profession 'full liberty to place their opinions before it.' But why was not the profession represented on the committee? And its opinions equally for your consideration as Minister? Would you not have had wiser and better advice for things that count over and above bureaucratic views and outside regulatory requirements? Will the opinions of the profession have any determining effect at this stage? To my mind, a real opportunity has been missed and an inferior future almost necessitated.
>
> Personally, I am ruled out of court. But the fact remains that I am a Senior Officer who served from first to last, who was called in to report at the worst stages not only to DMS Egypt but to yourself as Minister of Defence and who strove hard to improve conditions up to the finish at the recognised personal

risk and the usual personal cost. Since my return I have made my medical diary available for the Medical War Historian and openly and temperately brought the need for fundamental reforms before yourself as Minister, the Chief of Staff as your adviser, before the profession in both Congress and Council, and, as a last resource [sic], before the public. And nowhere or ever have my statements been challenged as untrue or not pertinent to the issue.

I accept official disregard as partly the price paid for the effort. But, in the interests and for the sake of the many who have suffered and will again suffer seriously and unnecessarily, I shall plead for a fuller and a wider review of the whole subject.

Can the matter fairly stand where it is?[10]

Ever polite, Pearce replied:

I regret that you do not approve of my action in regard to the personnel of the Committee of AIF Officers or of the scope of its duties, but I still feel that the Committee was thoroughly competent to advise the Government on the question submitted to it, ie., the reorganisation of the medical services of the CMF [Citizen Military Forces] in the light of war experience.[11]

The committee in question was chaired by Springy's wartime superior Sir Neville Howse, who in June 1921 had succeeded General Richard Fetherston as director-general of medical services in the post-war militia. The other members were Howse's close associates Colonel (later Major-General) Rupert Downes, Colonel (later Major-General) George Barber and Colonel (later Sir) Thomas Hurley. The committee undertook its work in January 1921 and delivered its report a year later, in February 1922. Recommendations accepted by the government were that the director-general of medical services position be made full-time, carry the rank of major-general, be open only to candidates with substantial war service, and be supported by a part-time deputy-director of medical services in each military district, as well as by professional officers responsible for dental, nursing, pharmaceutical and sanitation services. It also recommended better coordination of medical stores and supplies.[12]

Many of Springy's bitter criticisms of medical services at Gallipoli would probably not have arisen had these arrangements been in place in 1915. In many ways, the committee's recommendations can be seen as a vindication of his views, although he would never have been pleased unless things were done his way.

Feeling thwarted at the political level, Springy focused his attention on the Repatriation Department. He wrote to them, complaining of their poor assessment process, lack of necessary training, inhumane departmental policies on discharge, and inadequate pensions:

> There is ... a growing consensus of opinion that no case of functional nervous disease should be discharged from the Army until both his medical and social status have been finally determined, and that great loss is likely to accrue to both State and individual, whenever this rule is departed from. And yet the present War Office dictum is: 'Discharge as soon as possible'. If we, as experts, hold the opposite view, is it not incumbent upon us to place the non-military situation fairly and squarely before the authorities?
>
> Surely the proper way to regard Pensions is as the immediate financial side of Reconstruction or Repatriation (to use the Australian word). As such, they are fundamentally bound up with questions of treatment and training, and the sound principle is that of the alternative award in which the determining factors are the pre- war earnings and the present earning capacity. Speaking generally, a Pension should be a Statutory Right and not a mere grant. This is already the case in compensations for industrial disabilities under the Employers' Compensation Act, and much good, both direct and indirect, would inevitably follow a change in terminology in the case of disabilities incurred in war. Are not the War sufferers at least equally deserving?[13]

In response to his letter, Springy received a memorandum that questioned the basis of some of his assertions. To this he wrote a comprehensive response, stating that repatriation activities were the continuation and result of preventative and curative measures adopted by the Defence Department, referring to his own extensive experience and publications on the topic.[14] He was at pains to point out differing needs for differing problems, many of which were not properly dealt with, due to shortcomings in assessment and treatment by the department. Some problems were wholly due to war experiences, but others were superimposed upon pre-existing conditions:

> My statistics are that war conditions alone were sufficient to produce most confusional shell shock cases, that many neurasthenics and most psychasthenics had a pre-war vulnerability, and that the same applied to most epileptics—other than traumatic—and also to true psychoses. Many confusional cases, however, were long wrongly regarded and treated as insane, although they were really cases of emotional overthrow ... Confusional and true 'shell shock' cases will frequently continue to have a doubtful prognosis. Many psychical cases are distinguishable from petit mal only by no mental deterioration following. Traumatic epilepsy seems to have the same prognosis as in civil cases and, speaking generally, the same may be said of neurasthenia and psychasthenia ... All these cases, not only those in ease, but those in posse, and even all cases in doubt or who remain more or less dissatisfied, deserve and should receive a continuance of the best treatment, assistance and advice.[15]

He had previously emphasised the differing psychotherapeutic treatments needed for 'hysteroid' symptoms as opposed to the more generalised anxiety of 'shellshock', but now made additional comments on two other matters: psychotic disorders and epilepsy due to brain damage. He differentiated clearly between the large number sent to mental hospitals and the smaller proportion who actually suffered from psychotic illness:

> As official visitor to Metropolitan Asylums, and ex-medical officer, I have had special experience in Mental Diseases. The exact results of War strain and injury should be procurable from the statistical experience of such officers as Major Hollow of Mont Park Asylum, who could also give evidence as to the proportional number and prognosis of these who were, quite late in the War, sent in as mental; but who were really confusional. At the Front, the diagnosis 'mental' simply meant 'mental

symptoms, not yet fully diagnosed,' but it carried with it the sending of the patient to a Mental hospital, and frequently the more or less fixation of the cases as insane. It would be really only the late examinations of experts like Major Hollow whose results would be thoroughly reliable. My own experience both in England and here is to the effect that really mental cases were rarely due to War conditions unless (a) there was a family or personal history, or (b) a specific or similar taint lit up by injury or toxaemia.[16]

The emphasis on physical injury over psychological injury was also clear:

For some reason unknown to me, most of my cases this year have been of traumatic epilepsy, or other structural brain disease. I have had no case of stammering under treatment, and but a few cardiac or other neuroses. This has been a matter of regret to me since my main war and post war (at Mont Park) experience was in these directions. The head injuries of course call for one who is a neurological as well as a psychological expert, and traumatic epilepsy needs to be differently treated to idiopathic. It has also come under my notice that the replacement of bone over the trephine opening generally does harm rather than good.[17]

As well as discussing the obvious handicap of epilepsy immediately following head injury, he made a point of delayed-onset epilepsy, which could also have serious consequences in employment rehabilitation:

I have had a large number of such cases under treatment since 1916. Concussion cases may of course, become apparently normal though (following civil custom) develop Jacksonian [focal] epilepsy long after the original unconsciousness. Trephine cases [after skull surgery] will almost always have some disability, which will vary with the site and the severity— Traumatic Epilepsy, as a rule, is free from the progressive dementia of idiopathic epilepsy [of unknown cause, probably genetic], but it has almost the same industrial drawbacks. Only an occasional employer will give work after finding that the man 'takes fits'. I have elsewhere drawn attention to the unsatisfactory results following the transplantation of bone, and to the special industrial needs of this class of patients.[18]

Springy advocated employment rehabilitation for all the patients, but recognised that many would need special facilities, and some might not be able to be re-employed:

> With the co-operation of the Epileptic Colony and the Red Cross Society, we have accommodation for a few confirmed and badly situated cases at Masonmeadows. But this only meets the requirements of a special few and a special class. The majority being traumatic cases are best at home, or with friends if available, where of course, they still require treatment. The most difficult problem is the limited employment suitable and available. Few employers will keep on even a mild case. This raises the question whether some vocational school for epileptics might not be started to be more or less residential until otherwise determined.[19]

Springy then turned his attention to the matter of pensions:

> I have known many cases where Pensions were made below what I considered their physical and mental requirements. This was due, partly, to imperfect diagnosis, largely to faulty histories, and partly to the fact that the Pension Review was made without any knowledge or recognition of the then views of the attendant Medical Officer. At times there seemed to be an epidemic of reduced pensions, which it was difficult to justify from the Medical attendant's point of view.[20]

He recommended that no changes of pension should occur without consulting the medical practitioners concerned with the case. He also argued that pensions, employment training and social support were all essential components of humane care, and essential for obtaining the best possible treatment outcomes.[21]

Springy's onslaughts on the Repatriation Department did seem to have the desired effect, with a significant improvement in its handling of veterans, enabling him to devote more of his time to other tasks. He continued his twice-weekly outpatient work, mainly with traumatic epilepsy and shellshock cases, and each fortnight would visit a cottage at the Talbot Epileptic Colony, built by Red Cross, which he noted was 'practically originated by me and run upon my lines'. He represented the Returned Soldiers and Sailors League of Australia in the combined civil and military court cases dealing with mental patients at Mont Park, where he was pleased to note that cases the Repatriation Department accepted as caused by war service were given 'separate and admirable treatment'. Nevertheless, he believed there were many cases where veterans merited treatment but were missing out due to inadequate documentation.[22]

Amid all his battles with the Repatriation Department, Springy still had time for a couple more with different antagonists. One was with the Melbourne City Council over their decision to relocate the graves of some of Melbourne's earliest European settlers to make way for the Queen Victoria Market. *The Age* reported:

> A memorial service to the founders of Melbourne was held at the Melbourne Cemetery yesterday afternoon. Among those who gathered around John Batman's monument, where the service was held, was his great grandson, Mr Leslie Batman Weire.
>
> Dr J W Springthorpe stated that the occasion, besides being historic, was a mournful one, for the remains of the men who had made Melbourne were soon to be disinterred to make room for a market. (Shame). Sentiment, which should be most cherished in the minds of worthy people, was to be ruled apparently by vegetables. It was a discredit to the city. Here, in the cemetery, were the remains of John Charles King, the first Town Clerk, and of William Kerr, the second Town Clerk; the pioneers of Parliament, William Nicholson for instance, and pioneers of the civil service, and of practically every walk of life. All were to be sent to some obscure place, perhaps to Fawkner Cemetery. He deplored the fact that the monument of the founder of Melbourne, John Batman, was to be shifted, and that a vegetable market was to take its place. It was not, he added, the fault of the past but of the present generation.[23]

Although Springy was slightly mollified to hear that the Batman memorial and certain important graves were to move to the prominent site known as Flagstaff Hill, the protest offers a nice example of his essential conservatism.

Along with the poor treatment of veterans, Springy was concerned by Australia's high infant mortality rate. At the Intercolonial Medical Conference in Dunedin in 1896, he had been president of the Section of Public Health, which included papers by Dr Truby King (1858–1938). King was a New Zealand doctor who had trained in Scotland as a surgeon and physician but later specialised in psychiatry and child welfare, becoming the New Zealand Government's director of child health. He was credited with halving the infant mortality rate in New Zealand during his tenure, and his fame spread rapidly.

King emphasised a parenting style of discipline and detachment, implementing a strict routine of feeding, sleeping, toileting and child behaviour management. He encouraged breast-feeding with his slogan of 'breast fed is best fed', and in 1907 founded the Plunket Society (named after Lady Victoria Plunket, Governor of New Zealand) to apply scientific principles to the nutrition of babies. He established boarding facilities for infants at his Karitane residence near Dunedin, and a training scheme for 'Plunket Nurses'. These nurses, generally triple-certificated, highly trained and proud of their competence, were enthusiastic ambassadors for King's method.

Springy was fully attuned to King's eugenics, disciplinary approach, and scientific aspirations. He set up in Melbourne the Society for the Health of Women and Children, collaborating with Sister Maude Primrose, promoter of the Visiting Trained Nurses Association. Springy and Primrose, a graduate of King's infant welfare program, saw the opportunity to promote the Plunket system in Melbourne and thus reduce infant mortality and improve child welfare generally. The Plunket Sisters had centres in the working-class suburbs of Coburg and Footscray, but no place to train further double-certificated nurses in the methods of baby care that had proved so successful in New Zealand. Springy and Primrose approached philanthropic businessman Joseph Tweddle, a staunch Wesleyan Methodist, for financial support.

Dr Truby King Joseph Tweddle

Sister Maude Primrose Dr Vera Scantlebury Brown

Figure 36: (a) Dr Truby King (b) Mr Joseph Tweddle (c) Sister Maude Primrose (d) Dr Vera Scantlebury Brown

Although they initially thought of using Tweddle's property at Greensborough as the base of a training centre, it was ruled out as too remote. With the backing of the local council, who granted land, they decided to develop the centre at Footscray. Tweddle donated £3000 and guaranteed an overdraft up to £7000. The centre opened in 1920. Miss Moreland, one of Truby King's nursing sisters, was brought from New Zealand as matron of the Tweddle residential unit. She was so keen to improve conditions that she worked for at least the first six months without salary.

The Plunket centres directly competed with Victoria's baby health centres, which were set up by municipal councils, prompted by organisations such as the Country Women's Association. These outnumbered the Plunket centres tenfold and were also eager to establish a training school. They had the support of the Victorian Health Department under the principal child health officer, Dr Vera Scantlebury Brown, who favoured a much less rigid approach to parenting and childcare. Both organisations were making inroads into the high infant mortality rate, but the newspapers were only too happy to fuel the rivalry between the two movements.

During Truby King's 1919 visit to Melbourne, Springy's old colleague from Red Cross, Lady Helen Munro Ferguson, had summoned the two factions on an equal footing to Government House, in the hope that the prophet himself might resolve their differences. Although they reported agreement at the time, the schism continued. When Lady Helen returned to England in 1920, Lady Forster, wife of the new governor-general, withdrew her patronage from the Plunket Society and indicated her support for the rival baby health clinics. Later, Plunket received some financial support from the Victorian Governor's wife, Lady Stradbroke, and from the Victorian Government, but none from Lady Forster or the Federal Government. During a visit by Truby King ten years later, Dr Scantlebury Brown lamented: 'I wish he would go back to his little island and stay peacefully on his hill top'.[24] But the undeniable value of the Tweddle residential unit ensured its survival, and although it took several decades to reconcile with other providers, it still has an important place in the spectrum of services.

In the first few years after the war, Springy's financial stress remained significant. He asked his children to assist him financially, but they could not. On the contrary, in June 1923, Enid (now Mrs G. K. Totton) and her two children arrived from England after a near nine-year absence, and stayed for a year, during which time Springy supported them.[25] Also in 1923, Guy went overseas for postgraduate training and had to be supported.

Figure 37: John and Daisie at Joyous Gard

In his diary, Springy constantly referred with admiration to Daisie, who supported him in all he did. His great aim was to take her for a trip abroad, but with his diminishing finances, this seemed unlikely. Finally, he sold some land to raise the necessary funds, and in 1926 combined representing Victoria at the Sanitary Institute's Jubilee Congress and Conference on Child Welfare in London with an extensive holiday, covering England and Scotland, Italy and Switzerland, and a Mediterranean cruise.[26] While in London, Daisie was presented at court. They also went to the Derby, Kew Gardens, Windsor Castle, and the trooping of the colour rehearsal. Their cruise included Greece, Turkey, Egypt and Palestine, with a car trip from Haifa to Nazareth. They arrived home in August 1927.[27]

Before they left for overseas, Springy had chaired a committee raising funds for a memorial to Nurse Edith Cavell.[28] Cavell was an accomplished linguist, musician and artist, as well as a distinguished nurse. She had established a nursing school in Brussels, where she remained during the war to nurse wounded soldiers, some of them German. However, she was executed by German firing squad for her heroic efforts to help Belgian and other Allied refugees escape. Her self-sacrifice is an enduring inspiration for nurses everywhere.

The memorial is a white marble bust on a pedestal with reliefs typical of her life and death. It was unveiled on 11 November 1926 by Lieutenant-General Sir Harry Chauvel, Chief of the General Staff. An official guard and military band from Victoria Barracks attended. The memorial was originally on St Kilda Road, but was later relocated to Birdwood Avenue near the Shrine of Remembrance. The committee's appeal for funds met with such a generous response that, besides erecting the monument, it established a trust fund to help sick, needy and returned nurses.

The death of Sir Neville Howse in 1930 gave rise to a new wave of controversy. Howse had been appointed director-general of medical services (DGMS) in July 1921, while his committee considering the reorganisation of the Army Medical Service was still preparing its report. Michael Tyquin's biography of Howse described his struggles in dealing with military authorities, about which Springy had been so scathing. The committee's report gave him the belated opportunity to reduce those barriers:

> The committee's recommendations were a distillation of almost everything Howse had tried to achieve during the war. It proposed a full-time DGMS with the rank of major-general, a position that would be open only to those who had effective war service. It also suggested that this officer be present at any meeting of the Military Board when any question 'affecting the organisation, or administration of the medical services, or health of the troops, is being considered.' The committee sought direct access to the Minister by the DGMS if he believed such action was necessary. It also suggested a part-time support staff of at least five officers to be responsible for sanitation, dental, pharmaceutical, and nursing matters, the appointment of a DDMS in each military district to supersede the old PMO system, increased pay for medical officers (by 1 a day allowance for attending camps and training days) and free dental care for all members of the permanent forces.
>
> The Military Board approved most of the recommendations and agreed to look into others in the longer term. But it denied the DGMS direct access to the Minister.[29]

Howse held the position of DGMS for only sixteen months before he entered Federal Parliament as the National Party representative for the seat of Calare, which included his home city of Orange in western New South Wales. He remained a parliamentarian for the next seven years, and in that time served in the defence, health, repatriation and home and territories portfolios in the Bruce–Page coalition government. After losing his seat in the 1929 elections, he returned to his native England for a visit, and died there of cancer.

Many glowing obituaries were published, but one that referred to Howse as 'one of the best Directors of Medical Services of the war' particularly galled Springy. Unwisely, particularly given the very recent date of Howse's death, he responded in a long and damning letter to the *Medical Journal of Australia*. He criticised Howse's wartime record in vivid terms and praised his own efforts to rectify the many serious difficulties that Howse caused:

> Sir: 'De mortuis, nil nisi bonum' [of the dead, say nothing but good] is a worthy sentiment, only to be amended when far-reaching issues are involved and justice or hope make a contrary demand. Under these conditions I give my own experience at the war, from first to last, in many places and positions, as written from day to day in my diary, the 'ipsissima verba' of which are already in the hands of authorities and deposited in the Mitchell Library, corroborated as it has been in its main facts by the Official Historian, Colonel Butler, in Volume I of his history.
>
> Taking events in their sequence.
>
> I. As shown by Butler, the evolution of our
> 1. A.A.M.C. was poor and the mobilization of our A.I.F. unsatisfactory, both administratively and preventively. In my judgment it would have been much better developed if either Williams or Howse had remained behind and given Australia the benefit of their skill and experience.
>
> II. Both shared medical responsibility on the first convoy. Butler's account of medical happenings can scarcely be said to be to the credit of either.

III. At Mena Howse was in medical charge for some three or four strenuous months. As matters of fact, there were amounts and severity of sickness amazing amongst picked troops in a world-wide sanatorium during its season also; no provision for isolation, invaliding or convalescence, no facilities for dentistry or massage, latrines open, fly breeding unimpeded, and numerous unnecessary operations. On our arrival (3 A.G.H.) we found the RMO's complaining, the men underfed and overtrained, the camp improperly placed and our hospital tents being pitched in Nile-washed sand. Howse's greeting was: 'Whatever do you men want with an X ray outfit.' The amount of disease was astounding and ever increasing. There were few signs of catering for the 'humanities' and no sports, but full, unsupervised leave to Cairo, then more than ever a hotbed of vice and drugging. Whilst doing 'our jobs' remedially we were shocked, investigated and reported to all authorities. After unnecessary delay, the D.M.S. Egypt nominated an Australian Committee of Enquiry, of which, as senior, I was President. This met after the troops had left, and months later its report, condemnatory all round, was signed by two only out of its five members, myself and Captain Summons. In the course of time the camp itself was condemned. Worst of all, Howse had the reputation of 'knifing' anyone criticising or opposing, though 'the emotions rule the intellect' and may upset even the best laid schemes. And so it proved, later on.

IV. At Anzac Howse was mainly responsible medically from landing to evacuation. Butler's account is one terrible indictment, ending in 'medical failure.' True, the local obstacles were stupendous and the control both multiple and confusing. The '*Quicunque vult*' of the Athanasian Creed was translated into 'Whosoever will be promoted must believe the almost unbelievable.' Under such trying circumstances all agree that Howse showed great administrative activity, energy and endurance; but apparently he lacked foresight, insight and initiative and was too subservient to the Book of Regulations. At any rate, outsiders in Egypt, with little responsibility and less powers, felt it their duty to intervene. They sought to have transports manned for their own men by their own staff and to have Australian hospitals established in Alexandria. Neither was ever done. Nor did our general hospitals ever receive anything like their due proportion of bad cases, whilst many of the so-called 'septic' proved to be 'paratyphoid'. We found also that the early diarrhoeas were due to 'improper food,' not 'infection.' And our diagnosis was corroborated by the M.E.F. Advisory Committee, on which no place was ever found for even one Australian representative. Later on our hospitals in Egypt were crowded with diarrhoeal and dysenteric cases sent for treatment and convalescence to our torrid climate (in our kind egg albumen coagulated), a procedure for recommending [for] which I would have 'plucked' a student in Melbourne. And when the abdominal cases had invaded some two thirds of the men at Anzac, it was on our insistence that 'suitable foods' were forwarded and suitable Red Cross comforts—even Australia's 'Xmas gifts'— rushed to the front. Further, before the days of cold and blizzards, we sought to secure a 'winter ration', but were refused, apparently by the D.M.S. Egypt. In so far as he had the power and the foresight, calamities such as these, wherever arising from neglect or otherwise preventable, must be laid to the charge of Howse.

V. Meantime, in Egypt matters medical had become unbearable; junior officers, both R.A.M.C. and A.A.M.C., were doing their very best within the Regulations. But many of the senior R.A.M.C. resurrected under the exigencies of Kitchener's Army, had had a black mark placed against their names, 'never to be employed again'; yet such 'ruled the roost.' Our 2AGH was described as 'Woolloomooloo running Macquarie Street and Collins Street', whilst 1AGH had an able OC urged on by an ambitious 'all round expert.' Our OC., though S.M.O. [Senior Medical Officer], A.I.F., was always behind the times, whilst both the other leaders were ordered back to Australia and their extraordinary extensions condemned.

Thus 'Australia must have its own D.M.S., A.I.F.'—one who at least would carry weight, had experience and was energetic. The only man available was recognized to be Howse. After due consultation and many difficulties he was appointed and gazetted. Naturally he selected his staff temperamentally—two friendly consultants, three 'regulational' A.D.M.S. and a splendid first convoy Matron-in-Chief. Not unnaturally, the results were less satisfactory than was hoped and not lasting. The D.M.S. himself exerted little external power. And before all his staff, except the junior A.D.M.S. (also Staff Officer to the D.M.S. Egypt) left for the Western Front, our hospitals were again reporting to D.M.S. Egypt through one of his A.D.M.S., whilst no new consultants were appointed to take charge of what was left in Egypt, though suitable men were available to his knowledge. Hence, neither efficiency nor success warrant the eulogism, 'one of the best Directors of Medical Services at the war.' In my judgment, very far from it.

VI. As regards subsequent events—in Egypt, England and France—I defer comment until the appearance of Butler's next volume, in which he will, I hope, not only detail actual happenings, but also give official views re the praise or blame and tell Australia what, in his opinion, have been the main lessons of the war.

Meantime, it seems to me that the grim old Sphynx who, with wistful gaze, had watched his rising God flood Egypt and the Nile for thousands of years, must surely put on a look of surprise whenever he thought of the new nation that entered from the south, one of wonder when it proved itself 'the bravest thing God ever made,' and one of regret for the grave misfortunes that shrouded its dawn.

Yours, etc.,
J. W. Springthorpe. Lieutenant Colonel,
Australian Army Medical Corps. Melbourne.
December 17. 1930.[30]

Numerous responses praised Howse's work and criticised Springy's views, mainly along the lines that he had impossible expectations of what could have been done under the circumstances. Springy wrote further letters defending himself, saying that the respondents were not actually answering his criticisms – which were necessary to promote progress – but merely trying to stifle his freedom to speak. This prompted more furious responses, until the journal eventually shut down the correspondence. One of the last salvos came from Rupert Downes, Springy's old colleague in the army, on St John council, and on the Masseurs Registration Board (where he succeeded Springy as chairman). Downes referred to Howse as 'the most wonderful personality I have had the good fortune to meet'.[31] Springy's response (sent directly to Downes) said:

> You misjudge my objective, ignore facts and give no rebutting evidence and all in a tone that seems to me unnecessarily rude and even ungentlemanly.
>
> Of course, you had every incentive to speak up for your superior officer whom you knew so well. But that did not make it unfair for me to 'show up' what I regarded as defects. Specially under the justification of facts as quoted. Do you now offer any explanation?[32]

None was forthcoming.

In the last couple of years of his life, still preoccupied by the war and its aftermath, Springy wrote a play, titled *War's Awakenings*.[33] He said that his reason for writing it was based on his inclination towards prevention, rather than cure: 'So … I set myself to write a Play! Greek in spirit … but not in form. A Tragedy … though a Comedy would have been more attractive.'[34] A prologue introduced the characters responsible for England's entry and Australia's response. Three acts described his bêtes noires, with the incompetent British authorities and the medical officers facing overwhelming numbers of psychiatric casualties, not knowing what to do, and sending eighty per cent back to the lines, whereas only one per cent were fit. His Consultant persona prescribed the use of his record form to authorise repatriation of the psychiatrically ill back to England for expert treatment and, generally, home. An epilogue gave homilies on English ideals, the fighting spirit of the Australian soldiers, and the hope of the future in Rotarians, Truby King, boy scouts, Legacy movements, law and order, Junior Red Cross, and the League of Nations.

There is no record of the play ever having been performed, which is not surprising, given its stodgy, sermonic style. However, there is no doubt of Springy's sincerity in writing it, and it remains as a hologram of his sorrow.

Springthorpe died of cardiac and renal failure after a month at Epworth Hospital in Richmond, on 22 April 1933, aged seventy-seven. After his death, his body was taken home to Joyous Gard. Funeral services were conducted by Methodist ministers Rev. C. Irving Benson and Rev. E. Nye (chaplain of Wesley College) there and at Boroondara Cemetery, where he was buried in the family vault, alongside Annie and the infant Dorothy Anne. Obituaries were published in the *British Medical Journal* and *The Argus* (both of which incorrectly attributed his career to the Alfred Hospital), as well as in the *Medical Journal of Australia*, *The Herald* and *The Age*.[35]

The *British Medical Journal* focused on Springy's work on war neurosis, making the observation:

> As a thinker his reputation extended beyond his own city. In his Outline of Abnormal Psychology William McDougall refers to Springthorpe as one of the world authorities on this subject and mentions him among a group of the most eminent British physicians whose writings on psychology are well known.[36]

The *Age* obituary was a wide-ranging review of his achievements.[37] *The Argus* emphasised his support for dentistry and returned soldiers.[38] The *Medical Journal of Australia* gave the most comprehensive account of Springy's achievements. It mentioned, in particular, his work on tuberculosis, typhoid and psychological medicine, and his prolific participation in medical congresses. It highlighted his advocacy for better treatment of mental disorders and his extraordinary contributions to dentistry, nursing, physiotherapy and St John Ambulance. It then referred to his war service, his major contributions to the treatment of war neuroses, and his post-war work with repatriated soldiers and the epilepsy colony. It concluded with the following note:

> In addition to his many professional and public activities, Springthorpe was greatly interested in literature and art. He frequently contributed articles to the Press, and the year before his death published a play, 'War's Awakenings'. His collection of pictures and sculptures began at the time of the '9 × 4'

exhibition of Roberts, Condor and Streeton in the eighties. As well as examples of these masters, he possessed works by Bunny, Longstaff, Fox and Heysen; also of Bertram Mackennal's and Web Gilbert's sculpture. In his student days a good footballer and member of the old Toorak team, he was always an ardent advocate of amateur sport. He was President of the first amateur cycling body in Victoria, one time judge of the intercollegiate boat race and patron of the Medical Students' Hare and Hounds. For many years he was an active member of the Yorick and Wallaby Clubs, and of the Old Wesley Collegians' Association, of which he had been a member for sixty-one years.[39]

The journal's obituary was supplemented by three other contributions, one of which gave the opening lines of this book.

Springy left an estate valued for probate at £8280.[40] He was survived by Daisie, Enid, Lance and Guy.[41] Daisie died in 1966, aged eighty-two, and is also buried in the Springthorpe tomb.[42]

Much of Springy's art collection, and other contents of Joyous Gard, were sold at auction in May 1934. The 'Splendid furnishings of Late Dr. J. W. Springthorpe' mentioned in the Argus advertisement included pictures by Arthur Streeton, Hans Heysen, Blamire Young, Charles Conder, Janet Cumbrae Stewart, John Mather, Rupert Bunny, and Edward Cairns Officer, as well as *The Wheel of Life* by Web Gilbert and 'Old Work by Claude &c'.[43] The house and garden were demolished in 1935 to make way for suburban blocks. The great gates of the old Melbourne Hospital given to Springy in 1910, and used at Joyous Gard, were donated by Daisie to the local council. They now form the entrance to Springthorpe Park, which is opposite the Boyd Reserve in suburban Murrumbeena. The memorial plaque on the gate acknowledges the gift, but not the reason for it being there. Refer to Figure 38 on page 95.

For a man who achieved so much, it is interesting that he is so little recognised today. He is not mentioned at all in Michael Tyquin's monumental 684-page history of the Royal Australian Army Medical Corps.[44] He is mentioned briefly in Ian Howie-Willis's biography of Rupert Downes, but only in relation to his 'extraordinary attack' on Neville Howse, and I think this is the clue.[45] Springy was a formidable, divisive figure. Some people loved him, but others hated him.

Springy's deeply humanitarian ethos and his empathy for the underdog were overshadowed by his righteous indignation and personalisation of blame. If something was wrong, someone had to be held to account. His Methodist upbringing may account for these views, but his judgmentalism destroyed his reputation.[46]

Springy's work on post-war repatriation and the psychiatric care of veterans is commemorated by the name of the Springthorpe housing estate, which sprang up on the site of the old Mont Park and Bundoora Repatriation hospitals after they were decommissioned in the 1990s. Refer to Figure 39 on page 95. However, few people today know the reason for the name.[47] Were it not for the splendour of Annie's memorial, there would be little to remind us of the contributions of this remarkable man.

Notes

Notes to Chapter 1

[1] F. Meyer, 'Obituary of J.W. Springthorpe', *Medical Journal of Australia*, vol. 2, no. 1, 1 July 1933, p. 26.

[2] All the children of the family were Catherine (born and died 1854), Arthur (1854–1921), John William (1855–1933), Frederick George (1857–1902), Florence Mary (1860–1941), Amy Gertrude (1861–1877), Albert Henry (1863–1891), Edith Lucy (1864–1932), Charles Oscar (1867–1916), Frank Sydney (1870–1875), Kate (1872–1963), Edward Freeman (1873–1876), and Percy James (1882–1918). Sourced from: https://www.ancestry.com.au/family-tree/person/tree/113067276/person/142157562152/

[3] Table Talk, 'Coming men: No. 10: Dr J.W. Springthorpe', *Table Talk*, 16 June 1893, p. 3.

[4] Table Talk, 'Coming men: No. 10: Dr J.W. Springthorpe'.

[5] B. Egan, 'Springthorpe, John William (1855–1933)', *Australian Dictionary of Biography*, vol. 12, Melbourne University Press, 1990, pp. 38–9; Sydney Grammar School, 'SGS Liber Nominum 1857–1913', Sydney Grammar School, n.d., p. 279. https://www.sydgram.nsw.edu.au/community/school-archives/

[6] Meyer, 'Obituary of J.W. Springthorpe'.

[7] Springy retained his interest in 'Hare and Hounds', even when his running days were over. In 1890, for example, he offered a gold medal to the first hound in a race among medical students. 'The Hare and Hounds meet' is a very amusing unsigned article describing this in the Social Section of *Speculum: Journal of the Melbourne University Medical Students*, no. 21, June 1890, pp. 86–7.

[8] A. Sanders, 'Inner worlds: Less than six degrees of separation', video transcript of lecture delivered at the National Portrait Gallery, Canberra, 28 May 2011. https://www.portrait.gov.au/content/less-than-six-degrees-of- separation

[9] Sanders, 'Inner worlds'.

[10] The University of Melbourne, 'University of Melbourne Student Administration Archives', vols. 1877–79, University of Melbourne Archives, 1933.0049.

[11] F. Meyer, 'Obituary of J.W. Springthorpe', *Speculum: Journal of the Melbourne University Medical Students*, no. 132, May 1933, pp. 15–17.

[12] R. J. W. Selleck, *The Shop: The University of Melbourne 1850–1939*, Melbourne University Press, 2003, p. 149.

[13] Speculum, 'Report of the sub-committee *re* representation on senate', *The Speculum: A Journal of the Melbourne Medical Students*, no. 1, July 1884, pp. 8–9.

[14] Victoria Government Gazette, 'Acting medical superintendent, Beechworth Lunatic Asylum', *Victoria Government Gazette*, no. 23, 5 March 1880, p. 526.

[15] Egan, 'Springthorpe, John William (1855–1933)'.

[16] J. W. Springthorpe, 'Notes on twenty-one cases of epilepsy', *Australian Medical Journal*, vol. 8, no. 3, 15 March 1886, pp. 101–15.

[17] H. Edquist, 'Harold Desbrowe-Annear, the Springthorpe Memorial and the Arts and Crafts movement in Melbourne', *Fabrications: The Journal of the Society of Architectural Historians, Australia and New Zealand*, vol. 10, no. 1, August 1999, pp. 62–78.

[18] D. N. Mancoff, *The Return of King Arthur: The Legend through Victorian eyes*, Harry N Abrams, New York, 1995: 'The legend of King Arthur and his court at Camelot is one of the most enduring tales of Western culture. Born in the obscure past of dark-age Britain, Arthur created a kingdom governed by justice and generosity and protected by the most noble order of chivalric knights. This dream world of Camelot was celebrated generation after generation throughout the centuries. But Arthur's destiny was marked with tragedy. Corrupted by rivalry and betrayal, the peaceful kingdom fell to the ravages of war. Mortally wounded in battle, Arthur was taken by gentle queens to the Isle of Avalon to rest and heal until one distant day when his country would call for his return. With this promise of Arthur's return, the myth becomes a story without end, one that begs to be told again, and again. Wrapped in the mists of Avalon since the Middle Ages, the Once and Future King made his promised return in the nineteenth century.'

[19] Argus, 'Social', *Argus Supplement*, 19 June 1869, cited by J. R. Rudy in 'On Literary Melbourne: Poetry in the Colony, ca. 1854', *BRANCH: Britain, Representation and Nineteenth-Century History*, August 2012. https://branchcollective.org/?ps_articles=jason-r-rudy-on-literary-melbourne-poetry-in-the-colony-ca-1854

[20] H. McCrae, *Story-Book Only*, Angus & Robertson, Sydney, 1948.

[21] H. Attwood (ed), *The Centenary of the Wallaby Club, 1894–1994*, Landscape Publications, Melbourne, 1993, cited by G. McCarthy in 'History', *The Wallaby Club Inc.*, www.wallabyclub.org.au/compendium/biogs/E000263b.htm. Springy's friendships and interests certainly accord with the Yorick membership, although he is not mentioned in Thomas Carrington's reminiscences of the club, or in that book's lists of early or later members (Thomas Carrington, *The Yorick Club: Its Origin and Development, May, 1868 to December, 1910*, Atlas Press, Melbourne, 1911). His membership is claimed in *ADB* by Bryan Egan and in biographical notes by Volkhard Wehner in 'The story of the lost garden of Murrumbeena and its owners', 2008, State Library of Victoria, SLT 635 T79Y.

[22] Wehner, 'The story of the lost garden of Murrumbeena'.

[23] St John Ambulance Association, *St John Ambulance Association Annual Report*, St John Ambulance Association, Melbourne, 1886, p. 2.

[24] Argus, 'Births', *Argus*, 7 December 1887, p. 1.

[25] Sotheby's Australia, 'Unknown Tom Roberts portrait discovered', press release, 19 April 2016. https://www.smithandsinger.com.au/files/press/AU0806_ART_ROBERTS_ 20160511.pdf

[26] Herald, 'A question of medical etiquette' (editorial), *Herald*, 5 August 1887, p. 2.

[27] H. B. Allen, honorary secretary, Medical Society of Victoria, 'Notice to Dr John Springthorpe', 4 August 1887, reproduced in Herald, 'A question of medical etiquette'.

[28] Medico, 'Medico', letter to *Herald*, 8 August 1887, p. 3.

[29] Herald, 'Notes at the Medical Society's meeting', *Herald*, 11 August 1887, p. 3.

[30] Argus, 'The Melbourne Hospital', *Argus*, 19 August 1887, p. 6.

[31] Punch, 'Dr Springthorpe difficulty', *Punch*, 13 October 1887, p. 5.

[32] Undated newspaper cutting attributed as a leader in the *Daily Telegraph*, in File 1658, Microfilm 6356, Australian Medical Association Archives, Baillieu Library, University of Melbourne.

Notes to Chapter 2

[1] J. W. Springthorpe, 'Some points in the administration of anaesthetics', in *Transactions of the Intercolonial Medical Congress of Australasia, First Session, Held in Adelaide, South Australia, August–September, 1887*, Vardon and Pritchard, Adelaide, 1888, pp. 98–101.

[2] J. W. Springthorpe, 'The hepatic element of disease', in *Intercolonial Medical Congress of Australasia: Transactions of Second Session, Held in Melbourne, Victoria, January, 1889*, Stillwell & Co., Melbourne, 1889, pp. 67–71.

[3] See also J. W. Springthorpe, 'The etiology of acute rheumatism', *Intercolonial Medical Journal of Australasia*, vol. 5, no. 11, 20 November 1900, pp. 517–22 (reprinted by Stilwell & Co., Melbourne, 1900).

[4] J. W. Springthorpe, 'The nervous substratum of influenza', in *Intercolonial Medical Congress of Australasia: Transactions of Second Session, 1889*, pp. 101–5.

[5] J. W. Springthorpe, 'Some points of interest in the late epidemic', *Australian Medical Journal*, vol. 7, no. 10, new series, 15 October 1885, pp. 457–68.

[6] Springthorpe, 'The nervous substratum of influenza'.

[7] J. W. Springthorpe, 'A series of cases illustrating localisation in nervous diseases', in *Intercolonial Medical Congress of Australasia: Transactions of Second Session, 1889*, pp. 121–8.

[8] J. W. Springthorpe, 'Notes on typhoid fever', in *Intercolonial Medical Congress of Australasia: Transactions of Second Session, 1889*, pp. 173–5.

[9] H. N. MacLaurin, 'President's address: Comparative view of the mortality of the different colonies from certain diseases', *Intercolonial Medical Congress of Australasia: Transactions of Second Session, 1889*, pp. 401–33.

[10] J. W. Springthorpe, 'Hygienic conditions in Victoria', *Intercolonial Medical Congress of Australasia: Transactions of Second Session, 1889*, pp. 465–84 (reprinted by Stilwell & Co., Melbourne, 1889).

[11] J. Jamieson, 'Typhoid in Hobart and Melbourne, and the influence of drainage on its prevalence (read October 13th, 1902)', *Papers & Proceedings of the Royal Society of Tasmania*, 1902, pp. 95–9.

[12] Springthorpe, 'Hygienic conditions in Victoria'.

[13] J. W. Springthorpe, 'The medical aspect of tuberculosis', in *Intercolonial Medical Congress of Australasia: Transactions of the Fourth Session, Held in Dunedin, New Zealand, February, 1896*, printed by Otago Daily Times and Witness Newspapers, Dunedin, 1896, pp. 37–43.

[14] *Australasian Medical Gazette*, 'The case of the murderer Deeming'

(editorial), *Australasian Medical Gazette*, Sydney, 15 June 1892, pp. 260-2.

[15] J. Y. Fishbourne and J. W. Springthorpe, 'An account of the mental condition and trial of the Rainhill and Windsor murderer (Deeming alias Williams)', *British Medical Journal*, vol. 2, no. 1645, 9 July 1892, pp. 83-5.

[16] J. W. Springthorpe and W. L. Mullen, 'On the plea of insanity in criminal trials', in *Intercolonial Medical Congress of Australasia: Transactions of the Third Session, Held in Sydney, New South Wales, September, 1892*, Charles Potter, Government Printer, Sydney, 1893, pp. 647-64.

[17] Age, Letters to the editor, *Age*, 11, 12 and 21 October 1892.

[18] Springthorpe and Mullen, 'On the plea of insanity in criminal trials'.

[19] Springthorpe and Mullen, 'On the plea of insanity in criminal trials'.

[20] J. W. Springthorpe, 'Eighteen months' experience with tuberculin', in *Intercolonial Medical Congress of Australasia: Transactions of the Third Session, 1892*, pp. 165-7.

[21] J. W. Springthorpe, 'Presidential address to the Hygiene Section', in *Report of the Sixth Meeting of the Australasian Association for the Advancement of Science, held at Brisbane, Queensland, January 1895*, Australasian Association for the Advancement of Science, Sydney, 1895, pp. 73-182.

[22] J. W. Springthorpe, 'The beginnings of the Victorian Branch, B.M.A., 1879-1907', manuscript, 1907, MHM00676, Medical History Museum, University of Melbourne.

[23] T. S. Pensabene, *The Rise of the Medical Practitioner in Victoria*, Research Monograph 2, Australian National University, Canberra, 1980, pp.107-15.

[24] Congress Executive Committee, 'Report of executive committee', in *Intercolonial Medical Congress of Australasia: Transactions of the Fourth Session, 1896*, p. 3.

[25] Congress Executive Committee, 'Report of executive committee', p. 3.

[26] Springthorpe, 'The medical aspect of tuberculosis'.

[27] Springthorpe, 'The medical aspect of tuberculosis', p. 41.

[28] Springthorpe, 'The medical aspect of tuberculosis', pp. 40-1.

[29] J. W. Springthorpe, 'Tubercular disease in cattle', letter to *Brisbane Courier*, 18 January 1895, p. 2.

[30] Springthorpe, 'Tubercular disease in cattle'.

[31] C. Shoppee, in 'Conference at the City Hall. Tubercular diseases. Address by Dr Gresswell. Appointment of veterinary inspector recommended', *Ballarat Star*, 27 April 1896, p. 3, column 1.

[32] D. Whitley, C. Young, A. De Bavay, M. Cohen and J. W. Springthorpe, 'Pure milk supply for Victoria: Report of committee appointed at a meeting held

at the Royal Agricultural Society's rooms in Melbourne on the 6th day of August, 1896', *Australasian Medical Gazette: The Journal of the Australasian Branches of the British Medical Association*, vol. 15, October 1896, p. 500.

[33] W. A. Chapple, 'The public health aspect of alcohol', in *Intercolonial Medical Congress of Australasia: Transactions of the Fourth Session, 1896*, pp. 291–303.

[34] W. M. Stenhouse, reported in 'The public health aspect of alcohol', in *Intercolonial Medical Congress of Australasia: Transactions of the Fourth Session, 1896*, p. 300.

[35] J. W. Springthorpe, reported in 'The public health aspect of alcohol', in *Intercolonial Medical Congress of Australasia: Transactions of the Fourth Session, 1896*, pp. 302–3.

[36] W. M. Stenhouse, 'Educational problems affecting health', in *Intercolonial Medical Congress of Australasia: Transactions of the Fourth Session, 1896*, pp. 304–7.

[37] Stenhouse, 'Educational problems affecting health'.

[38] Otago Witness, 'Intercolonial Medical Congress of Australasia: Fourth Session 1896: Report on proceedings of the Section of Public Health', *Otago Witness*, no. 219, 20 February 1896, p. 23.

[39] J. W. Springthorpe, 'The battle of life' (Section of Public Health: President's Address), in *Intercolonial Medical Congress of Australasia: Transactions of the Fourth Session, 1896*, pp. 267–76.

[40] Springthorpe, 'The battle of life', p. 270.

[41] Springthorpe, 'The battle of life', pp. 275–6.

[42] F. C. Batchelor, cited in 'The battle of life', *Otago Witness*, 13 February 1896, p. 23.

[43] J. W. Springthorpe, 'Report of Dr J.W. Springthorpe, representative of Victoria, Public Health Section, Intercolonial Medical Congress, Dunedin', 29 February 1896, in Film 6356, File 1549, microfilm archival collection of Australian Medical Association, Baillieu Library, University of Melbourne.

[44] The report of the event said: 'The lawns proved to be in capital order, notwithstanding the rain which had fallen in the morning, and large numbers of ladies and gentlemen were able to enjoy to the full the pleasure of strolling on the lawns and through the club grounds. Refreshments were served during the afternoon, and the committee of the club were indefatigable in their efforts to promote the enjoyment of their guests.

Altogether the garden party was most enjoyable and will be remembered as not the least brilliant of the social gatherings which will mark the meeting of the Medical Congress in Dunedin.' Otago Witness, 'Intercolonial Medical

Congress: The Fourth Session', *Otago Witness*, 6 February 1896, p. 22.

[45] Otago Daily Times, 'The medical picnic to the higher alps', *Otago Daily Times*, 17 February 1896, p. 3.

[46] J. W. Springthorpe, 'Review of reviews. Dr Springthorpe, 20 December 1895', cited in K. Dunstan, *The Confessions of a Bicycle Nut*, Information Australia, Melbourne, 1999, pp. 55–7.

[47] Dunstan, *The Confessions of a Bicycle Nut*, pp. 55–7; A. L. Booth, *Riding High: Burston & Stokes Centenary Ride, 1888–1988*, Bicycle Victoria, Melbourne, 1988, p. 2.

[48] Launceston Examiner, 'Intercolonial news items', *Launceston Examiner*, 15 February 1895, p. 5.

[49] Argus, 'An amateur cycling union', *Argus*, 31 March 1897, p. 7.

[50] Argus, 'Cycling: Victorian Amateur Cyclists' Union', *Argus*, 16 June 1897, p. 7.

Notes to Chapter 3

[1] J. W. Springthorpe, 'Personal diaries', vol. 1 1883 – vol. 14 1931, State Library of Victoria.
[2] Springthorpe, 'Personal diaries', vol. 2, entry for 8 September 1898.
[3] This is Professor Pat Jalland's thesis in a study of Victorian attitudes towards the afterlife. Jalland writes: 'Springthorpe's grief and commemoration of Annie was an extreme form of the traditional Christian culture of death and bereavement inherited from Britain ... As a devout Protestant, the 42-year-old widower initially sought consolation in his Christian belief in a God who made possible immortality and reunion in the afterlife. The morning after Annie's death Springthorpe took the Christian sacrament and made a sacred vow to dedicate his life to God and to Annie. He vowed in his diary to remain "ever faithful to her dear self in body and soul—so that at the last— we may be reunited in love for evermore". This sacred vow helps to explain the gap of almost twenty years before he married again, in an age when wealthy middle-aged widowers often married younger women after only two years or so of bereavement. / Springthorpe's scientific reasoning conflicted with his Christian hopes for a future reunion with Annie, as he agonised in his diary about the nature and conditions of heavenly reunions. He needed physical evidence, but though Annie was immortal: "She has come no nearer—No miracle—No Farewell! No Voice from Beyond. / Simply an icy silence". / Ultimately the prospect of an undefined and highly conditional reunion with Annie was elusive, unfulfilling, and outside Springthorpe's control. He turned instead to the concept of memory in his quest for more satisfying ways of perpetuating Annie's influence and ensuring that her life lived on. / The energetic and highly practical "Springy" required an elaborate and multi-faceted process of tangible memorialisation that he could lovingly create and supervise. / He explored all the more traditional forms of middle-class commemoration, such as hair rings, photographs and grave-visiting. The most fulfilling sites of his grief and mourning in the first year of bereavement were his diary and the Collins Street house he had so happily shared with Annie and the children. The private diary was the site where he mentally worked through his grief and his memories and carefully planned his practical commemoration, while also continuing with his thriving Collins Street medical practice.' P. Jalland, 'Magnificent obsession', *The Age*, 25 March 2002. https://www.theage.com.au/entertainment/art-and-design/magnificent-obsession-20020325-gdu2rs.html

[4] Springthorpe, 'Personal diaries', vol. 1, 1896.

[5] J. W. Springthorpe, with illustrations by J. Longstaff, *In Memoriam: Annie Constance Springthorpe*, privately published, Melbourne, 1897. Copy held in Baillieu Library, University of Melbourne.

[6] Jalland, 'Magnificent obsession'; A. Sanders, 'Springthorpe, John William (1855–1933)', in Christopher Chapman (ed) *Inner Worlds: Portraits & Psychology*, exhibition catalogue, National Portrait Gallery, Canberra, 2011, pp. 119–22; J. Rizzetti, 'Love and death: The Springthorpe memorial at Boroondara (Kew) Cemetery', *The Resident Judge of Port Phillip* [blog], 3 January 2013. http://residentjudge.wordpress.com/2013/01/03/love-and-death-the-springthorpe-memorial

[7] Springthorpe, 'Personal diaries', entry for 26 February 1897.

[8] Springthorpe, 'Personal diaries', entry for 4 October 1898.

[9] G. Down, 'Stained glass', in A. B. May and S. Swain (eds), *The Encyclopedia of Melbourne*, Cambridge University Press, Melbourne, 2005, pp. 683–84.

[10] J. Lis, *The Love That Never Dies: The Secret Symbolism of the Springthorpe Memorial*, 17-page pamphlet, Joseph Lis, Morwell, Victoria, 2018, p. 10.

[11] This remarkable monument has been extensively described by various authors, some of whose words I have used, including Edquist, 'Harold Desbrowe-Annear, the Springthorpe Memorial and the Arts and Crafts movement in Melbourne'; Jalland, 'Magnificent obsession'; Rizzetti, 'Love and death'.

[12] As Jalland writes: 'The turning of the first sod for the foundations in 1899 forced Springthorpe to consider an unwelcome thought, which he seemed to have been pushing to the back of his mind; the erection of the mausoleum meant that Annie's body would have to be re-interred. He reassured himself: "It is necessary, otherwise it would not be done, but it can be carried out without any jarring of feeling." / He could not repress the thought that he had the opportunity to gaze upon her "earthly form" again, though he well knew what he would see. But he thrust the idea away, on the grounds that he no longer associated her spirit with her former physical body, any more than with her "dear remembered garments, ornaments" or even her lock of hair in his ring. He determined to include the children in the re-interment ceremony, to provide another link "in the chain of memory and affection". / So, on July 19th, 1899 he made up bouquets for the children to place on the coffin in the open vault while he read an appropriate service. If other people found this re-interment ceremony at all macabre, it appeared to affect him little; as he was leaving space in the tomb for the children, they needed to be

associated with its erection' (Jalland, 'Magnificent obsession').

[13] Kew Cemetery, RES A 0001 30/12/1887, relocated to SPEC A 001 19/7/1899.
[14] Springthorpe, 'Personal diaries', vol. 3, entry for 2 October 1899.
[15] Springthorpe, 'Personal diaries', vol. 3, entry for 9 February 1901.
[16] Springthorpe, 'Personal diaries', vol. 3, entry 10 February 1901.
[17] *The Bulletin*, cited in Rizzetti, 'Love and death'.
[18] The Lone Hand, 'Australian Art, 1908: Victorian Artists' Exhibition', *The Lone Hand*, 1 October 1908, p. 637. https://nla.gov.au/nla.obj- 390679136/view?sectionId=nla.obj-428331323&partId=nla.obj- 402321953#page/n44/mode/1up
[19] R. Marginson, interviewed by R. Sloggett, 'Sculpture in the grounds, with some memories of things that got away', *University of Melbourne Collections*, no. 9, December 2001, p. 4.
[20] Table Talk, 'A home and garden that is out of the ordinary', *Table Talk*, 1 January 1925, pp. 29–30.
[21] M. Tuckett, *A year in my garden*, Melville & Mullen, 1905, reprinted together with Wehner, 'The story of the lost garden of Murrumbeena'.
[22] Argus, 'Splendid furnishings of late Dr. J. W. Springthorpe' (advertisement), *Argus*, 5 May 1934, p. 2.
[23] Marginson, interviewed by Sloggett, 'Sculpture in the grounds', p. 4.

Notes to Chapter 4

[1] Australasian Medical Gazette, 'Victorian Branch of the British Medical Association', *Australasian Medical Gazette*, 20 April 1900, pp. 158–66.

[2] Argus, 'Medical etiquette: Mr. H.M. O'Hara's position discussed by the British Medical Association', *Argus*, 22 March 1900, p. 6.

[3] Australasian Medical Gazette, 'The O'Hara case' (letter to the editor), *Australasian Medical Gazette*, 20 August 1900, p. 341.

[4] Pensabene, *The Rise of the Medical Practitioner in Victoria*, pp. 107–15.

[5] Australian Trade Union Archives, 'Royal Victorian Trained Nurses Association (1904–1934)', in *Australian Trade Union Archives*. https://www.atua.org.au/biogs/ALE1056b.htm

[6] J. W. Springthorpe, 'Circular letter from the council of the RVTNA to members of committees of management, matrons and teaching staff of all registered training schools', 21 June 1905, reported in Victorian Trained Nurses' Association, *UNA: The Journal of the Victorian Trained Nurses' Association*, vol. 3, no. 4, 1905, p. 56.

[7] M. Grehan, 'Professional aspirations and consumer expectations: Nurses, midwives, and women's health', PhD thesis, School of Nursing and Social Work, University of Melbourne, 2009, pp. 183–98.

[8] J. W. Springthorpe, cited in Grehan, 'Professional aspirations and consumer expectations', pp. 183–98.

[9] Springthorpe, 'Circular letter'. The circular read as follows: 'Ladies and Gentlemen, / The Council of the Royal Victorian Trained Nurses' Association takes this opportunity of thanking you for invaluable co-operation in the work of establishing a uniform system of training and examination for Nurses throughout Victoria. The result has been so generally satisfactory that the Association has had the title "Royal" conferred upon it by His Most Gracious Majesty, King Edward VII., and its position has been highly commended by nursing authorities at home and abroad. If, however, its efficiency is to be all that it may and can be, it still requires to advance in the direction of a uniform standard of preliminary training and education, some extension of the schedule study, and some satisfactory scheme for securing the special fitness of its future Matrons. / These matters have been under careful consideration for some twelve months past, during which the Council has benefitted by valuable information from the different local Training Schools, by the practice and aims of the best Training Schools elsewhere, and by the co-operation of the Australasian Trained Nurses' Association, the Director of Education

of Victoria, and the Australian Health Society. / The outcome of their joint labours has been the enclosed circular, which received the approval of the Council at its last meeting. In connection therewith, your special attention is drawn to the following: / (a) The educational standard now required is a State one, open to everyone, and within the capacity of average intelligence. It is not to be compulsory for 3 years, but preferential (other qualifications being equal). The procedure is that already adopted in most of our Training Schools, and in vogue in the best elsewhere. / (b) The preliminary training now recommended is specially adapted to the work of the Nurse, is of State efficiency and extent, and within the powers of the average probationer. It also will be preferential, and not compulsory for 3 years. / (c) The additions to the nursing curriculum are simply desirable extensions, and fulfilments of what is already in the schedule of study. / (d) The certificate of Technical fitness for future Matrons is similarly well calculated to render future Matrons specially qualified for their work, both as regards the Hospital and the Training School. / Adequate provision also has been made for the practical carrying out of all recommendations and requirements. No vested right is infringed, and no hardship is entailed upon any one. / The Council, therefore, has confidence in anticipating your continued help and co- operation, along these lines of advancing efficiency. / I have the honor to be, / Ladies and Gentlemen, / Your most obedient servant, J.W. SPRINGTHORPE, President.'

[10] J. W. Springthorpe, 'Letter of thanks', published in October 1905 issue of *UNA*, the magazine of the Royal Victorian Trained Nurses Association: 'Through the mysterious and friendly offices of Dr Meyer, it has taken the exact form, that of a library standard works for my children, which I should have chosen had I been made aware of your kindly intentions. It is extremely gratifying to me to be thus assured that the labour of love undertaken on behalf of Victorian nursing has been appreciated, and in my "Nurses' Library" I shall always be reminded that the efforts which I have been privileged to make have not been in vain.'

[11] Although the term 'physiotherapy' emerged in the mid-nineteenth century, Australian practitioners only changed the name of the Australian Massage Association (AMA) to the Australian Physiotherapy Association (APA) in 1938.

[12] As quoted in J. W. Springthorpe, *Therapeutics, Dietetics and Hygiene: A Text-Book*, 2 vols., James Little, Melbourne, 1914.

[13] Springthorpe, *Therapeutics, Dietetics and Hygiene*.

[14] J. McMeeken, *Science in our Hands: Physiotherapy at the University of*

Melbourne 1895–2010, Faculty of Medicine, Dentistry and Health Sciences, University of Melbourne, 2018, p. 49.

[15] The report of the meeting said: 'After letters from medical men throughout the Commonwealth expressing sympathy with the movement had been read, it was unanimously decided to form an association, to be the recognised association of the profession throughout the Commonwealth.

The objects are to establish a system of registration of acknowledged medical masseurs and masseuses, to establish a uniform system of training and examination, to be of such standard as may be decided on by the medical profession and the executive of the association, and to promote the interests of the massage profession in all matters appertaining to its work. The following provisional committee, to frame a constitution, was appointed:—Chairman. Dr. Springthorpe; and Drs. MacGillicuddy and MacGibbon, Messrs. Grundt, Best, Pascal, Peters, Robertson, Doyle, Kyte and Moody, Mesdames Frokjar, Hacke and Vahland, with Misses M'Cauley, Robertson, Meares and Mortyn, together with the following Inter-State representatives:—Messrs. Schuch (New South Wales), Senmens and Leshan (South Australia), Alex. Peters (Western Australia), and Peterson (Tasmania). Mr. Best, of the Alfred Hospital, was elected treasurer pro tem., and Mr. Teepoo Hall (Melbourne Hospital) secretary.' L. S. Chipchase et al., 'Looking back at 100 years of physiotherapy education in Australia', *Australian Journal of Physiotherapy*, vol. 52, no. 1, 2006, pp. 3–7.

[16] Chipchase et al., 'Looking back at 100 years of physiotherapy education in Australia'.

[17] McMeeken, *Science in our Hands*, p. 61.

[18] McMeeken, *Science in our Hands*, p. 63.

[19] J. McMeeken, 'Australian physiotherapists in the First World War', *Health and History*, vol. 17, no. 2, 2015, pp. 52–75.

[20] Herald, 'Cycling', *Herald*, 18 March 1905, p. 5.

[21] University of Melbourne, 'Minutes of council of University of Melbourne', 6 March 1905, reported in A. Mawdsley, 'A medical man supporting the dental profession', in J. Healy (ed), *Dentistry: Innovation and Education*, Henry Forman Atkinson Dental Museum, University of Melbourne, 2020, p. 148.

[22] A fellow member of the Dental Board, Dr J. G. Nihill, recalled: 'I was closely associated with him in all his efforts, which resulted in the recognition by the Melbourne University of dentistry as a profession. At first, after a course of study of two years, the dental student obtained the diploma of Member of the Australian College of Dentistry. Later, the status of the dentist was improved

by extending the curriculum and granting the diploma of L.D.S. and the degrees of B.D.S. and D.D.S.' J. G. Nihill, 'Obituary of Dr J.W. Springthorpe', *Medical Journal of Australia*, vol. 2, no. 1, 1 July 1933, p. 28.

[23] Dental Students' Society, 'Report of annual dinner, Dental Students' Society', University of Melbourne Archives, Faculty of Dentistry 1904–1927, 7 December 1904, 2000/0123.

[24] Argus, 'Obituary. Dr J.W. Springthorpe: Long record of service', *Argus*, 24 April 1933, p. 8.

[25] Australian Town and Country Journal, 'Deaths', *Australian Town and Country Journal*, 15 October 1902, p. 20.

[26] Sydney Morning Herald, 'Metropolitan District Court. Wednesday, Lantsberry v. Vicery and another', *Sydney Morning Herald*, 13 October 1892, p. 7.

[27] New South Wales Government Gazette, 'Chief Secretary's Office, Sydney, 29th June, 1897', *New South Wales Government Gazette*, 29 June 1897, p. 4377, item 11814.

[28] Sydney Morning Herald, 'Funeral of Mr. Fred. G. Springthorpe', *Sydney Morning Herald*, 14 October 1902, p. 6.

[29] Punch, 'People we know', *Punch*, 26 September 1907, p. 6.

[30] Springthorpe, 'Notes on twenty-one cases of epilepsy'.

[31] J. W. Springthorpe, 'Treatment of epilepsy by removal of peripheral irritants', *Australian Medical Journal*, vol. 9, no. 4, 15 April 1887, pp. 177–80.

[32] J. W. Springthorpe, 'Notes on fifty cases of epilepsy', *Australian Medical Journal*, vol. 10, new series, 1888, pp. 3–6.

[33] Springthorpe, 'Notes on fifty cases of epilepsy', p. 6.

[34] P. F. Bladin, 'The history of epilepsy in Victoria', in J. Chambliss, M. Cook and J. Healy (eds), *Epilepsy: Perception, Imagination and Change*, exhibition catalogue, Medical History Museum, University of Melbourne, 2014, p. 24–6.

[35] E. L. Zox (chair), *Royal Commission on Asylums for the Insane and Inebriate*, Government of Victoria, 1886.

[36] J. W. Springthorpe, 'Epileptic colony', letter to *Argus*, 5 August 1905, p. 15.

[37] Kalgoorlie Miner, 'A condemnatory report: Disgraceful state of affairs', *Kalgoorlie Miner*, 23 August 1902, p. 5.

[38] Age, 'The asylum scandal: High-handed action of the chief secretary', *Age*, 12 August 1902, p .4.

[39] Age, 'A strong protest', *Age*, 23 August 1902, p. 9. Dr Beattie-Smith was also a Fellow of the Royal College of Surgeons, so some reports give the appellation 'Mr', although most say 'Dr'.

[40] Age, 'Kew Asylum scandal: Dr Springthorpe's investigation', *Age*, 20 August 1902, p. 7.
[41] Age, 'A strong protest'.
[42] Age, 'Dr Springthorpe's investigation', *Age*, 20 August 1902, p. 7.
[43] Argus, 'Asylum doctors: Dr Springthorpe's findings', *Argus*, 23 August 1902, p. 13.
[45] Age, 'Our lunatic asylums: The need for reform', *Age*, 26 August 1902, p. 5.
[46] Age, 'A strong protest'.
[47] Argus, 'Asylum doctors: Mr Beattie-Smith's position', *Argus*, 26 August 1902, p. 5.
[48] Age, 'Our lunatic asylums: The need for reform'.
[49] Age, 'The Lunacy Bill: Some important reforms', *Age*, 2 September 1902, p. 4.
[50] Age, 'Lunacy reform: Indifferent medical supervision', *Age*, 1 September 1902, p. 5.
[51] Age, 'Asylum doctors: Report by Drs Jamieson and Joske, *Age*, 29 August 1902, p. 5.
[52] Age, 'The asylum scandal: Inquiry demanded by the medical officer', *Age*, 2 September 1902, p. 4.
[53] Age, 'State political notes', *Age*, 4 September 1902, p. 4.
[54] Age, Leading article, *Age*, 8 September 1902, p. 4.
[55] J. V. McCreery, *Hospitals for the Insane: Report of the Inspector of Lunatic Asylums 1902*, Government of Victoria, Melbourne, 1903.
[56] The Lunacy Department (located in the Chief Secretary's Department) was established in 1905 under the provisions of the *Lunacy Act 1903*. This department was the main agency responsible for the care, control and treatment of persons who were deemed to be 'lunatics', 'idiots' (later 'mental detectives'), 'inebriates' or 'criminally insane' and of 'persons suffering a mental disorder arising from war service'. The department was also responsible for administering hospitals and licensed houses for the insane. Before the establishment of the Lunacy Department, the Hospitals for the Insane Branch (Chief Secretary's Department) had been the agency responsible for these functions and the chief administrative officer had been the Inspector of Lunatic Asylums and Licensed Houses. Under the provisions of the *Lunacy Act 1903*, public asylums became known as 'hospitals for the insane'. This change of name reflected a change in emphasis, from detention and custody to treatment and rehabilitation, which had been evolving since the mid-nineteenth century. Hospitals for the insane were for the care and

control of long-term patients. The Act also provided for the establishment of receiving houses to which patients were admitted for observation, diagnosis and short-term treatment. Lunacy wards in public hospitals became used for the temporary reception of insane persons or persons presumed to be insane. The Act also authorised the proclamation of separate institutions for the criminally insane and privately run institutions known as licensed houses. The *Inebriates Act 1904* reintroduced a system of licensed premises for the reception, control and treatment of inebriates. (Source (edited): Public Record Office Victoria, 'Lunacy Department (located in Chief Secretary's Department): Public Record Office Victoria', Australian Research Data Commons. https://researchdata.edu.au/lunacy-department-located-secretary039s-department/490179)

[57] E. Cunningham Dax, 'John William Springthorpe: A remarkable physician', in *'Outpost Medicine': Australasian Studies on the History of Medicine; Third National Conference of the Australian Society of the History of Medicine*, University of Tasmania and the Australian Society of the History of Medicine, Hobart, 1993, p. 271: 'The most forceful of his works is a paper read at a meeting of the Medical Society of Victoria in 1903. In it he denounced the government for the insufficient staff, the deficient medical and surgical equipment, the structural defects, the excessive restraint, the insanitary overcrowding, and the lack of classification of the patients. It was subsequently agreed that Drs. Springthorpe, Fishbourne and Beattie Smith be invited to confer with the Medical Society to make a deputation to meet the Chief Secretary ... Between 1885 and 1910 Springthorpe had a vast influence for good upon the mental health services. He exposed the dreadful conditions and restraints in the asylums and greatly influenced the promulgation of the 1903 Lunacy Act. He attempted to raise the standards of treatment by suggesting that general hospitals should open beds for early cases of mental illness and that receiving houses and observation wards be built or opened in country areas. To achieve these ends he made fearless onslaughts upon his opponents, the Chief Secretary, the Public Service Board, Dr Ernest Jones (Head of the Mental Health Department), Sir James Barrett, himself a formidable figure, and the Master of Lunacy ... He was, undoubtedly, among the most remarkable and energetic medical men in Melbourne at the turn of the century ... and one of the greatest medical reformers in Victoria.'

[58] University of Melbourne, 'Minutes of university council, 1904', Ref. [21209-000252], University of Melbourne Archives, 2000.0099.

[59] Age, 'University of Melbourne: Senior public and junior commercial

examination', *Age*, 25 January 1909, p. 5.

[60] A. Sanders, Response to Rizzetti, 'Love and death', 30 December 2013, viewed 25 August 2020. https://residentjudge.com/2013/01/03/love-and-death-the-springthorpe-memorial-at-boroondara-kew-cemetery/

[61] Table Talk, 'A home and garden that is out of the ordinary', p. 29.

[62] Table Talk, 'A home and garden that is out of the ordinary', p. 29.

[63] Table Talk, 'Weddings: Mr. Merric Boyd to Miss Doris Gough', *Table Talk*, 21 October 1915, p. 9. Guy Springthorpe is listed among the guests.

[64] K. Russell, *The Melbourne Medical School, 1862–1892*, Melbourne University Press, 1977, pp. 110–11.

[65] Springthorpe, *Therapeutics, Dietetics and Hygiene*.

[66] J. W. Springthorpe, 'Inaugural lecture, Melbourne Hospital Clinical School, session 1890', *Australian Medical Journal*, vol. 12, no. 4, 15 April 1890, pp. 149–61 (and reprinted by Stilwell & Co., 1890).

[67] Russell, *The Melbourne Medical School*.

[68] Springthorpe, *Therapeutics, Dietetics and Hygiene*, p. 121.

[69] Springthorpe, 'Inaugural lecture', pp. 149–61.

Notes to Chapter 5

[1] Springthorpe, *Therapeutics, Dietetics and Hygiene*, p. 608.
[2] Springthorpe, *Therapeutics, Dietetics and Hygiene*, p. 8.
[3] D. Pride, 'The viruses inside you', *Scientific American*, vol. 323, no. 6, December 2020, pp. 38–45.
[4] Springthorpe, *Therapeutics, Dietetics and Hygiene*, p. 44.
[5] Springthorpe, *Therapeutics, Dietetics and Hygiene*, p. 41.
[6] Springthorpe, *Therapeutics, Dietetics and Hygiene*, p. 15.
[7] N. W. Gillham, 'Sir Francis Galton and the birth of eugenics', *Annual Review of Genetics*, vol. 35, December 2001, pp. 83–101.
[8] Springthorpe, *Therapeutics, Dietetics and Hygiene*, p. 38.
[9] Springthorpe, *Therapeutics, Dietetics and Hygiene*, p. 44.
[10] Springthorpe, *Therapeutics, Dietetics and Hygiene*.
[11] Springthorpe, *Therapeutics, Dietetics and Hygiene*, p. 640.
[12] Springthorpe, *Therapeutics, Dietetics and Hygiene*, p. 130.
[13] Springthorpe, *Therapeutics, Dietetics and Hygiene*, p. 132.
[14] J. W. Springthorpe, 'The tactus eruditus' (paper delivered to Intercolonial Medical Congress, Auckland, 1914), *Australian Medical Journal*, 28 February 1914, pp. 1450–1 (reprinted by Shipping Newspapers, Melbourne, 1914).
[15] Springthorpe, *Therapeutics, Dietetics and Hygiene*, p. 9.
[16] Springthorpe, *Therapeutics, Dietetics and Hygiene*, p. 608.

Notes to Chapter 6

[1] National Archives of Australia: Australian Imperial Force; B2455, First Australian Imperial Force Personnel Dossiers, 1914–1920; Springthorpe John William : Service Number - Lieutenant Colonel : Place of Birth - Wolverhampton England : Place of Enlistment - N/A : Next of Kin - (Wife) SPRINGTHORPE Mrs, 1914–1920, p. 1 of 30.

[2] J. W. Springthorpe, 'Diary of the war 1914–1919: Medical extracts', note of 17 September 1917, Medical History Museum, Faculty of Medicine, Dentistry and Health Sciences, University of Melbourne, MHM00677.

[3] Dr MacAdam was a fellow lecturer for St John Ambulance Association.

[4] Guy was now seventeen years of age.

[5] Punch, 'Au revoir to Dr Springthorpe', *Punch*, 10 December 1914, p. 34. The article concluded: 'Among those invited were: Dr. Springthorpe, Mr. and Mrs. Syme, Mrs. S.T. Staughton, Dr. and Mrs. Stirling, Miss Lesley Madden, Mr. F. Tricks, Dr. and Mrs. F. Newman, Dr. and Mrs. Davies, Dr. and Mrs. Leon Jona, Mr. and Mrs. Hardie, Dr. and Mrs. MacAdam, Dr. and Mrs. Lambert, Dr. Constance Ellis, Dr. Hamilton, Dr. Margaret Mac Loranin, Dr. Denehy, Dr. King-Scott, Mr. Ormond, Dr. S. W. Talbot, Miss O'Connor, Dr. and Mrs. Lillies, Dr. Maudsley, Dr. and Mrs. Dunhill, Dr. and Mrs. Davenport, Dr. Newton, Col. and Mrs. Burston, Dr. and Mrs. Felix Meyer, Dr. and Mrs. Ormond, Mr. and Mrs. Chas. Moore, Mr. and Mrs. M'Crea, Master Guy Springthorpe, Mrs. Paterson, Mr. W. H. Paterson, Misses Rose and Aimee Paterson'.

[6] The College of Surgeons later became the Royal Australasian College of Surgeons.

[7] Daily Telegraph, 'H.C.W., 'Melbourne doings', *Daily Telegraph*, 30 June 1915, p. 6;
Punch, 'Approaching marriages', *Punch*, 27 May 1915, p. 27.

[8] Herald, 'In the public eye: Men and women. Personal paragraphs', *Herald*, 22 May 1913, p. 12.

[9] Argus, 'Births', *Argus*, 23 February 1918, p. 13.

[10] Springthorpe, 'Diary of the war', entry for 16 December 1914.

[11] NAA: B2455, Springthorpe John William, p. 21 of 30.

[12] Springthorpe, 'Diary of the war', entry for 5 December 1914.

[13] The tenth Hague Convention of 1907 had adapted to maritime warfare the principles of the Geneva Convention of 1906.

[14] Major-General Sir William Bridges KCB, CMG (1861–1915), founder and

inaugural commanding officer of Royal Military College, Duntroon, was the first Australian chief of general staff. He commanded the 1st Australian Division at Gallipoli, where he died on 18 May 1915. C. Clark, 'Bridges, Sir William Throsby (1861–1915)', *Australian Dictionary of Biography*, vol. 7, Melbourne University Press, 1979.

[15] Major-General (later Sir) William Williams KCMG, KStJ (1856–1919) had been principal medical officer in the New South Wales colonial army and was appointed inaugural Director of Army Medical Services after Federation. A. J. Hill, 'Williams, Sir William Daniel Campbell (1856– 1919)', *Australian Dictionary of Biography*, vol. 12, Melbourne University Press, 1990.

[16] C. E. W. Bean, *Official History of Australia in the War of 1914–1918. Volume 1: The Story of ANZAC from the Outbreak of War to the End of the First Phase of the Gallipoli Campaign, May 4, 1915*, 11th edn, Angus & Robertson, Sydney, 1941, pp. 64–140. Grand Cordon of the Order of the Rising Sun (Japan) Field Marshal William Riddell Birdwood, 1st Baron Birdwood, GCB, GCSI, GCMG, GCVO, CIE, DSO (1865–1951) was a British Army officer. He had seen active service in the Second Boer War in the staff of Lord Kitchener.

[17] Springthorpe, 'Diary of the war', entry for 13 January 1914.

[18] Springthorpe, 'Diary of the war', entry for 24 January 1915.

[19] Springthorpe, 'Diary of the war', entry for 25 January 1915.

[20] Springthorpe, 'Diary of the war', entry for 5 December 1915.

[21] A.G. Butler (ed), *Official History of the Australian Army Medical Services in the War of 1914–1918; Vol. 1, Gallipoli, Palestine and New Guinea*, Australian War Memorial, Canberra, 1930, p. 404.

[22] Springthorpe, 'Diary of the war', entry for 30 January 1915.

[23] Bell tents are low, circular, poorly ventilated, made of heavy canvas and constructed around a central pole. They are better suited to cold climates than to desert heat.

[24] Springthorpe, 'Diary of the war', entry for 8 April 1915.

[25] Springthorpe, 'Diary of the war', entry for 8 April 1915.

[26] Springthorpe, 'Diary of the war', marginal note to entry for 8 April 1915.

[27] Springthorpe, 'Diary of the war', entry for 8 April 1915.

[28] Butler (ed), *Official History of the Australian Army Medical Services*, p. 199.

[29] Springthorpe, 'Diary of the war', marginal note to entry for 11 April 1915.

[30] Springthorpe, 'Diary of the war', entry for 29 April 1915.

[31] Springthorpe, 'Diary of the war', entry for 6 May 1915.

[32] Springthorpe, 'Diary of the war', entry for 8 May 1915. This comment in parentheses is in the uninterrupted typescript but appears to have been added

in the interval between handwriting the diary and its subsequent typing, as it is not a marginal comment.

[33] Springthorpe, 'Diary of the war', entry for 9 May 1915.

[34] Springthorpe, 'Diary of the war', entry for 28 May 1915.

[35] Springthorpe, 'Diary of the war', entry for 7 June 1915.

[36] S. Murray-Smith, 'Barrett, Sir James William (1862–1945)', *Australian Dictionary of Biography*, vol. 7, Melbourne University Press, 1979.

[37] Springthorpe, 'Diary of the war', entry for 25 January 1915.

[38] Springthorpe, 'Diary of the war', entry for 7 June 1915.

[39] Springthorpe, 'Diary of the war', entry for 7 June 1915.

[40] Springthorpe, 'Diary of the war', entry for 9 June 1915.

[41] Springthorpe, 'Diary of the war', entry for 16 June 1915.

[42] Springthorpe, 'Diary of the war', entry for 25 July, plus marginal note.

[43] Springthorpe, 'Diary of the war', entry for 15 June 1915.

[44] J. W. Springthorpe, 'Letter to Lady Helen Munro Ferguson', 28 June 1915, cited in Justice J. F. Kershaw, *Report of Committee of Enquiry to Investigate Charges Against Lieutenant Colonel Barrett in Connection with the Australian Branch of the British Red Cross Society*, 4 January 1916, p. 11 (report held among Springthorpe's papers at the Australian War Memorial, Canberra, Collection 2DRL/0701, Series 2/1).

[45] Springthorpe, 'Letter to Lady Helen Munro Ferguson', 28 June 1915.

[46] M. Rutledge, 'Knox, Sir Adrian (1863–1932)', *Australian Dictionary of Biography*, vol. 9, Melbourne University Press, 1983.

[47] J. W. Springthorpe, 'Letter to Lady Helen Munro Ferguson', 15 July 1915, cited in Red Cross 'Field Force Report on Sir James Barrett', held in papers of the Australian Red Cross Society, National Office, Correspondence files, National Headquarters, 1914–1955, Unit 203, University of Melbourne Archives, 2015.0033.

[48] J. W. Springthorpe, 'Letter to Lady Helen Munro Ferguson', 13 July 1915, cited in Red Cross 'Field Force Report on Sir James Barrett'.

[49] J. W. Springthorpe, 'Letter to Lady Helen Munro Ferguson', 23 August 1915, cited in Red Cross 'Field Force Report on Sir James Barrett'.

[50] Herald, 'Red Cross scandal: Disgraceful chaos alleged', *Herald*, 6 September 1915, p. 10.

[51] Herald, 'Red Cross Society: James W. Barrett and Dr. Springthorpe …', *Herald*, 11 September 1915, p. 11.

[52] Herald, 'Red Cross Society: James W. Barrett and Dr. Springthorpe …'.

[53] Herald, 'Dr. Barrett to return: Recall order to operate', *Herald*, 7 September

1915, p. 8.
[54] Herald, 'Better control needed for Red Cross work: Parliamentary action urged', *Herald*, 15 September 1915, p. 1.
[55] Herald, 'Red Cross dispute: Dr. Springthorpe's charges still remain unanswered', *Herald*, 18 September 1915, p. 9.
[56] Kershaw, *Report of Committee of Enquiry*.
[57] Springthorpe, 'Diary of the war', entry for 11 October 1915.
[58] A. G. L. Shaw, 'Argyle, Sir Stanley Seymour (1867–1940)', *Australian Dictionary of Biography*, vol. 7, Melbourne University Press, 1979.
[59] Kershaw, *Report of Committee of Enquiry*, p. 6.
[60] Kershaw, *Report of Committee of Enquiry*, Addendum.
[61] Kershaw, *Report of Committee of Enquiry*, p. 8.
[62] On the first point, it said that Springy had failed to prove Barrett had 'taken control', because responsibility had been delegated by General Williams, and Barrett was clearly not responsible for all the difficulties. On the second point, it said that Ordnance was primarily responsible for supplies and that supplementary Red Cross comforts 'could not' have been landed (notwithstanding Springy's evidence that British Red Cross had been able to do so for British troops). On the third point, it said that military medical services were responsible, not Red Cross, and certainly not Lieutenant-Colonel Barrett. On the fourth point, it said that Ordnance was primarily responsible, not Red Cross, and 'comforts' could have been requested from Red Cross whenever desired. It cited Springy's own success at doing this as evidence that it was his own fault, not Barrett's, that the problem remained. On the fifth point, it showed that Red Cross supplies were provided on some ships, thereby disproving Springy's assertion that troops on transports were neglected, and stated, 'It will be seen that Lieut. Colonel Springthorpe's charges in respect of these transports fall to the ground'. Kershaw, Report of Committee of Enquiry, passim.
[63] Kershaw, *Report of Committee of Enquiry*.
[64] Kershaw, *Report of Committee of Enquiry*, p. 56.
[65] Kershaw, *Report of Committee of Enquiry*, p. 47.
[66] Kershaw, *Report of Committee of Enquiry*.
[67] Springthorpe, 'Diary of the war', entry for 3 January 1916.
[68] Reported in *The Age* on 14 January 1916, p. 7, as a communication from the O/C, Intermediate Base, Egypt.
[69] *The Age*, 14 January 1916, p. 7.
[70] NAA: B2455, Springthorpe John William, p. 21 of 30.

[71] Springthorpe, 'Diary of the war', entry for 23 January 1916.

[72] J. W. Springthorpe, 'The great withdrawal—Story of a daring plan—Last days at ANZAC—How our soldiers left', *Age*, 1 February 1916, pp. 7–8.

[73] J. W. Springthorpe, 'Australians at Anzac—Lecture by Col. J.W. Springthorpe', *Age*, 15 March 1916, p. 10.

[74] NAA: B2455, Springthorpe John William, p. 28 of 30.

[75] Argus, 'Deaths … Springthorpe', *Argus*, 24 April 1933, p. 1.

[76] Western Mail, 'A woman's Melbourne letter', *Western Mail*, 31 March 1916, p. 38.

[77] Springthorpe, 'Personal diaries', vol. 8, entry for 16 March 1916.

[78] Marriage 2964/1916, BDM Victoria.

[79] Jessie continued to work for the Boyds until her death at Joyous Gard on 31 May 1922 (Argus, 'Deaths … Johnstone', *Argus*, 2 June 1923, p. 13). She was buried in the Inglis family gravesite at Boroondara Cemetery.

[80] NAA: B2455, Springthorpe John William, p. 28 of 30.

[81] Age, 'Red Cross. The Central Council. Help for the French. Melbourne, Wednesday', *Age*, 16 March 1916, p. 8.

[82] J. W. Springthorpe, 'Red Cross Administration in Egypt' (letter to the editor), *Age*, 17 March 1916, p. 8.

[83] Medical Journal of Australia, 'The case of Lieutenant-Colonel Barrett' (editorial comment), *Medical Journal of Australia*, vol. 1, no. 21, 20 May 1916, pp. 418–19.

[84] Handwritten note in introduction to Kershaw, *Report of Committee of Enquiry*.

[85] Springthorpe, 'Diary of the war', entry for 16 March 1916.

[86] G. R. McR., 'Obituary: R. Markham Carter, C.B., F.R.C.S., D.T.M.', *British Medical Journal*, 25 March 1961, p. 908.

[87] M. Oppenheimer, *The Power of Humanity: 100 Years of Australian Red Cross 1914–2014*, HarperCollins, Sydney, 2014, pp. 38–40.

[88] Oppenheimer, *The Power of Humanity*, pp. 38–40.

[89] Oppenheimer, *The Power of Humanity*, pp. 38–40.

[90] NAA: B2455, Springthorpe John William, p. 7 of 30.

Notes to Chapter 7

[1] NAA: B2455, Springthorpe John William, p. 8 of 30.
[2] Springthorpe, 'Diary of the war', entry for 2 October 1916.
[3] Springthorpe, 'Diary of the war', entry for 4 October 1916.
[4] Springthorpe, 'Diary of the war', entry for 11 October 1916.
[5] Springthorpe, 'Diary of the war', entry for 30 October 1916.
[6] Springthorpe, 'Diary of the war', entry for 18 December 1916.
[7] Springthorpe, 'Diary of the war', entry for 15 January 1917.
[8] Springthorpe, 'Diary of the war', entry for 25 January 1917.
[9] Springthorpe, 'Diary of the war', entry for 25 January 1917.
[10] Springthorpe, 'Diary of the war', entry for 15 July 1917.
[11] Springthorpe, 'Diary of the war', entry for 20 March 1917.
[12] Springthorpe, 'Diary of the war', entry for 15 July 1917.
[13] Springthorpe, 'Diary of the war', entry for 20 July 1917.
[14] Springthorpe, 'Diary of the war', entry for 20 July 1917.
[15] Springthorpe, 'Diary of the war', entry for 12 April 1917.
[16] McR., 'Obituary: R. Markham Carter'.
[17] Springthorpe, 'Diary of the war', entry for 13 April 1917.
[18] The stripe was first authorised under Army Order 204 of 6 July 1916: 'The following distinctions in dress will be worn on the service dress jacket by all officers and soldiers who have been wounded in any of the campaigns since 4th August, 1914:—Strips of gold Russia braid, No. 1, two inches in length, sewn perpendicularly on the left sleeve of the jacket to mark each occasion on which wounded', and was refined by Army Council Instruction No. 2075 of 3 November 1916: '1. The term "wounded" refers only to those officers and soldiers whose names have appeared or may hereafter appear in casualty lists rendered by the Adjutant General's office at a base overseas, or by the G.O.C. any force engaged in active operations. Reports in hospital lists are not to be regarded as authoritative for this purpose.'
[19] Springthorpe, 'Diary of the war', entry for 19 September 1917. See also B. K. Rank, *Jerry Moore and Some of his Contemporaries*, Hawthorn Press, Melbourne, 1975, which says of Springy that 'it was an open secret that owing to his persistence and against the wishes of the British Headquarters Staff, the death penalty for alleged cowardice on duty was never inflicted on Australian soldiers' (p. 84).
[20] Springthorpe, 'Diary of the war', entry for 22 November 1917.
[21] Springthorpe, 'Diary of the war', entry for 24 November 1917.

[22] Springthorpe, 'Diary of the war', marginal note to entry for 28 November 1917. He discussed this card and included an example in his conference paper 'Suggestions as to the better treatment of our war neuroses' in *The Inter-Allied Conference on the After-Care of Disabled Men: Second Annual Meeting; Held in London, May 20th to 25th, 1918. Reports Presented to the Conference*, His Majesty's Stationery Office, London, 1918, pp. 258–64. https://archive.org/stream/interalliedconfe00interich/interalliedconfe00interi ch_djvu.txt Dr Reginald Jeffery Millard was a medical practitioner from Sydney who served with the Australian Army Medical Corps from 1914 to 1919. Before the outbreak of World War I, he was medical superintendent at the Coast Hospital (later Prince Henry Hospital) in Little Bay, Sydney. In July 1915, he was promoted to lieutenant-colonel, and in early 1916, he became Assistant Director of Medical Services at Australian Imperial Force Headquarters. In January 1917, now a colonel, Millard went to France to command the No. 1 Australian General Hospital at Rouen.

[23] Springthorpe, 'Diary of the war', entry for 16 January 1918.

[24] Springthorpe, 'Diary of the war', entry for 16 January 1918.

[25] Springthorpe, 'Diary of the war', marginal note to entry for 15 February 1918.

[26] Springthorpe, 'Diary of the war', marginal note to entry for 13 April 1918.

[27] Springthorpe, 'Diary of the war', entry for 19 February 1918.

[28] Springthorpe, 'Diary of the war', entry for 21 February 1918.

[29] Punch, 'Fact and rumour', *Punch*, 21 February 1918, p. 26. The nature of the illness was not reported, and was not noted in Springy's personal diary.

[30] Springthorpe, 'Suggestions as to the better treatment of our war neuroses'. He discussed the assessment card subsequently used during repatriation.

[31] Springthorpe, 'Diary of the war', entry for 27 May 1918.

[32] Springthorpe, 'Diary of the war', entry for 27 May 1918.

[33] Springthorpe, 'Diary of the war', entry for 29 May 1918.

[34] Springthorpe, 'Diary of the war', entry for 10 June 1918.

[35] Springthorpe, 'Diary of the war', marginal note to entry for 29 May 1918.

[36] Springthorpe, 'Diary of the war', entry for 22 June 1918.

[37] NAA: B2455, Springthorpe John William, p. 28 of 30.

[38] Springthorpe, 'Diary of the war', entry for 13 August 1918.

[39] NAA: B2455, Springthorpe John William, p. 9 of 30.

[40] Springthorpe, 'Diary of the war', entry for 12 December 1918.

[41] 'Cuckoo', 'Melbourne letter', *Critic*, 5 February 1919, p. 21.

[42] Argus, 'Age moratorium. Dr. Springthorpe's claim', *Argus*, 25 March 1919, p. 4.

Notes to Chapter 8

[1] J. W. Springthorpe, 'War neuroses and civil practice', *Medical Journal of Australia*, vol. 2, no. 14, 4 October 1919, pp. 279–84.
[2] Springthorpe, 'War neuroses and civil practice', p. 281.
[3] Springthorpe, 'Diary of the war', postscript.
[4] Springthorpe, 'Diary of the war', postscript.
[5] Springy wrote these in his lectures for medical students, referred to them in his diary postscript, then presented them as a paper, 'Psychology and medicine', in *Transactions of the Eleventh Session Australasian Medical Congress Held in Brisbane, Queensland, 21st–28th August, 1920*, A.J. Cumming, Government Printer, Brisbane, 1921, p. 404. His paper was printed in several journals, including *The Lancet* (1920), *The Journal of Nervous and Mental Disease* (1921) and the *Medical Journal of Australia* (1922).
[6] J. W. Springthorpe, 'After-care of disabled soldiers', Australian War Memorial archives, 2DRL/0701/Series 5/ Wallet 2 of 7. See also 'Letter to Repatriation Commission', 14 July 1920, re treatment of cardiac and neurological (and mental) cases.
[7] Springthorpe, 'Suggestions as to the better treatment of our war neuroses'.
[8] J. W. Springthorpe, 'Some lessons of the war', *Australasian Medical Congress: Transactions of the Eleventh Session, Held in Brisbane, Queensland, 21st–28th August, 1920*, also Australian War Memorial archives, 2DRL/0701/Series 3/ Wallet 3 of 3.
[9] NAA: MP367/1, 527/2/177.
[10] National Archives of Australia: Department of Defence; MP367/1, General correspondence files, 1917–1929; 527/2/177, Lieutenant Colonel JW Springthorpe - Comments on medical services, 1920–1921.
[11] NAA: MP367/1, 527/2/177.
[12] Australian Army Medical Services, *Report of the Committee appointed to advise upon the re-organization of the Australian Army Medical Services*, 1922, AWM 54, 481/2/29.
[13] NAA: MP367/1, 527/2/177.
[14] J. W. Springthorpe, 'Memorandum to deputy commissioner', Department of Repatriation, 10 July 1922. Australian War Memorial, 2DRL/0701/ Series 5, Wallet 2 of 7. He cited his publication 'The better treatment of our war neuroses' in the transactions of the Aftercare Inter-Allied Conference, London, May 1918, as well as in papers on 'Twelve months at the front' and 'War neuroses and civil practice' in the *Medical Journal of Australia* and in

papers on 'Some lessons of the war', 'The treatment of war neuroses' and 'Cardiac neuroses and their treatment' forwarded to the Australian Medical Congress held in Brisbane in 1920.

[15] Springthorpe, 'Memorandum to deputy commissioner'.

[16] Springthorpe, 'Memorandum to deputy commissioner'.

[17] Springthorpe, 'Memorandum to deputy commissioner'.

[18] Springthorpe, 'Memorandum to deputy commissioner'.

[19] Springthorpe, 'Memorandum to deputy commissioner'.

[20] Springthorpe, 'Memorandum to deputy commissioner'.

[21] Springthorpe, 'Memorandum to deputy commissioner'.

[22] Springthorpe, 'Diary of the war', postscript.

[23] Age, 'Is sentiment dead?' *Age*, 23 January 1922, p. 8.

[24] V. Scantlebury Brown, 'Diary B4', 12 February 1929, p. 73, cited by P. M. Smith in 'Mothers and babies: Aspects of infant survival; Australia 1880–1950', PhD thesis, Australian National University, Canberra, 1990, p. 189. On Scantlebury Brown's work generally, see H. Sheard, *A Heart Undivided: The Life of Dr Vera Scantlebury Brown*, Faculty of Medicine, Dentistry and Health Sciences, University of Melbourne, 2016.

[25] Herald, 'Social circle', *Herald*, 18 July 1923, p. 13.

[26] Springthorpe, 'Personal diaries', vol. 10, 1922–26. The two blocks of land were from a wilderness area at the edge of Joyous Gard that Springy called his 'forest'. He had intended to bequeath Joyous Gard wholly to his daughter, Enid. When he first contemplated selling the land, in a diary entry dated 1 January 1923, he said, 'Enid willing!' However, as his financial stress continued and there was no letter from Enid for more than six months, he appears to have made a unilateral decision. A diary entry dated 8 March 1923 reports the first block sold for £1350. A diary entry dated 6 April 1923 reports the second block sold for £1125.

[27] Springthorpe, 'Personal diaries', vol. 10, 1922–26.

[28] Wehner, 'The story of the lost garden of Murrumbeena'.

[29] M. B. Tyquin, *Neville Howse: Australia's First Victoria Cross Winner*, Oxford University Press, Melbourne, 1999, p. 135.

[30] J. W. Springthorpe, 'The war and Sir Neville Howse's part therein', letter to the *Medical Journal of Australia*, vol. 1, no. 5, 31 January 1931, p. 155.

[31] R. Downes, letter to the *Medical Journal of Australia*, 14 March 1931, cited in I. Howie-Willis, *Surgeon and General: The Life of Major General Rupert Downes*, Australian Military History Publications, Australia, 2008, p. 249.

[32] J. W. Springthorpe, letter to Rupert Downs, 31 January 1931, Australian

War Memorial, Springthorpe Collection 2DRL/0701, Series 5, Wallet 7.

33 J. W. Springthorpe, *War's Awakenings: Wise and Otherwise; A Tragedy in a Prologue, Three Acts and an Epilogue, by "A Digger"*, printed (for the author) by J. L. Anderson & Sons Pty Ltd, Melbourne, 1932.

34 J. W. Springthorpe, 'War's awakening': presidential address to the Society for the Health of Women and Children, 23 August 1932.

35 Herald, 'Dr J. Springthorpe: Burial at Kew today', *Herald*, 24 April 1933, p. 2.

36 British Medical Journal, 'Obituary: J.W. Springthorpe, M.D., M.R.C.P., physician, Alfred Hospital, Melbourne', *British Medical Journal*, vol. 2, no. 3786, 29 July 1933, p. 216.

37 Age, 'Well-known physician. Death of Dr. Springthorpe. An interesting career', *Age*, 24 April 1933, p. 8.

38 Argus, 'Dr. J.W. Springthorpe: Long record of service'.

39 Medical Journal of Australia, 'Obituary, J.W. Springthorpe', *Medical Journal of Australia*, vol. 2, no. 1, 1 July 1933, pp. 26.

40 In 2020, as a multiple of average weekly earnings, this would value the estate at a little over $3 million. (See *MeasuringWorth*, https://www.measuringworth.com/calculators/australiacompare/relativevalue.php, viewed July 2021.)

41 Howie-Willis, *Surgeon and General*.

42 Ian Howie-Willis reminded me that Springy was one of Melbourne's leading Methodist laymen, at a time when religious affiliation was important, and being Methodist was a very honourable thing. The pervasiveness of the Wesleyan outlook is encapsulated in the rhyme 'I'm Methody born and Methody bred, and when I'm gone that's a Methody dead!'

43 Argus, 'Deaths ... Springthorpe'.

44 M. B. Tyquin, *Little by Little: A Centenary History of the Royal Australian Army Medical Corps*, Army History Unit, Department of Defence, Canberra, ACT, 2003.

45 'Kew Cemetery: Find a grave', https://www.kewcemetery.com.au/search/FindGrave.php, viewed 27 September 2021.

46 Argus, 'Splendid furnishings of late Dr. J.W. Springthorpe'. See also Argus, 'Springthorpe collection Australian pictures' (advertisement), *Argus*, 22 May 1934, p. 2.

47 In 1993, the Victorian State Government established the Bundoora–Mont Park Reference Group (or BMPRG) to provide recommendations for the future development of the area. In 1995, as much of the Mont Park Hospital precinct was decommissioned, the BMPRG presented its 'Master Plan for the Future'. This envisaged six to eight hundred new dwellings in

the Gresswell–Mont Park–Plenty area (depending on the extent of La Trobe University's requirements for the site). The landscape architectural practice of Mark McWha P/L was engaged in 1999 to prepare a landscape master plan. This included the obligation to retain all 'Heritage Listed' aspects of the former Mont Park Hospital precinct, as well as a number of other 'heritage sensitive' aspects of the site. This included preserving many of its majestic trees. The urban design practice of Taylor Cullity Lethlean completed the detailed design of the Estate to '… create a unique environment featuring exclusive designs, natural setting and an integrated solution to housing'. The spine of the estate is Springthorpe Boulevard and one of its features is the Springthorpe Country Club. The design was presented with multiple Urban Development Institute of Australia 'Awards for Excellence' in 2003 and 2004 for its Urban Renewal. (G. Cotchin, 'Mont Park to Springthorpe … from hospital grounds to a housing estate', *Mont Park to Springthorpe: Springthorpe Heritage Project*, n.d. https://www.montparktospringthorpe.com/mont-park-to-springthorpe-from- hospital-grounds-to-a-housing-estate/)

INDEX

A

A'Beckett, Emma	3
Alfred Hospital	5, 23, 59, 161, 176
Alfred, Prince	2, 59
Allbutt, Sir Clifford	138
Andrew, Professor Henry Martyn	8, 75
Argyle, Stanley	113, 185
Arthurian legends (and King Arthur)	6, 79
Asylums, official visitor	65, 67, 70-75, 147
Australian Association for the Advancement of Science	34, 84
Australian Massage Association	61, 62, 108, 175 See also 'Physiotherapy'
Australian Red Cross	106, 108-119, 121-125, 129-132, 137, 149-150, 153, 158

B

Barrett, Lt-Col. James	80, 106-119, 122-123, 179
Beattie-Smith, Dr William	58, 71-75
Beechworth asylum	4, 165
Boyd, Arthur Merrick	3, 80
British Medical Association, Victorian Branch	9-10, 25, 30-34, 57-58
Brown, Dr Vera Scantlebury	152-153, 190
Burnet, Sir Macfarlane	39

C

Camelot	6, 12, 13, 26-27, 48, 51, 98, 121, 165
Carter, Lt. Col. R. Markham	123, 125, 132
Cemetery Memorial at Boroondara	12, 46, 51-54, 161, 172

Committee of Enquiry (Kershaw)	113-124
Constitution ("nature")	33, 86-87
Cycling	44-46, 62, 162

D

Darwin, Charles	29, 87
Dax, Dr Eric Cunningham	75, 179
Deeming case	30-32, 167
Deakin, Alfred	31
Dentistry	33, 62-64, 109, 157, 161
Desbrowe-Annear, Harold	6, 51-52, 165, 172
Downes, Colonel Rupert	145, 106, 162

E

Education	36, 40, 42, 87-90, 174
Epilepsy	67-68, 80, 147-150, 161
Epileptic colony	67-70, 79, 149-150, 161
Eugenics	34, 42, 88, 151, 181

F

Ferguson, see Munro-Ferguson	
Fink, Theodore	6
Fishbourne, Dr JWY	31, 57, 67, 71, 168, 179
Ford, General	99, 102, 106, 107
Forster, Lady	153
Fort Street School	2
Freud, Sigmund	80, 133

G

Galton, Francis	87-88
Ghezireh Hospital	102, 105-106
Gilbert, Web	54, 80, 162
Greswell, Dr Dan	38, 75, 168, 192
Guilfoyle, William	51, 79

H

Hall, Teepoo	61
Hare and hounds	2, 162, 164

Henry, Dr Louis	9
Howse, Sir Neville	99-102, 110, 121, 130-131, 137-38, 145, 155-58, 160, 162

I

Iliffe, John	62
Inglis, Annie	3, 6, 10-12, 44-51, 92, 171
Inglis, Edgar	2
Inglis, Florence	46, 79
'In Memoriam' book	48-51
Intercolonial Medical Congress	23, 32-35, 90, 151

J

Jackson, Dr John Hughlings	65, 148
Johnstone, Daisie	79, 120-121, 138, 154, 162
Johnstone, Jessie	79, 120, 121
Joyous Gard	6, 55, 79-80, 98, 121, 154, 161-162, 190

K

Keogh, Sir Adrian	101, 131
Kershaw, His Honour, Judge J.	113, 184-185
King Arthur	see Arthurian legends
King, Dr Truby	151-153, 160
Knox, Adrian	110-112, 123, 184
Koch, Dr Robert	29-30

L

Longstaff, John	6, 12, 48, 162, 172
Luna Park	103-104

M

Mackennal, Bertram	3, 6, 51, 53, 94
Massage, see Physiotherapy	
Maudsley, Dr Henry	22, 58, 80
Maudsley Hospital	127, 133
Medical Board of Victoria	22
Medical Society of Victoria	5, 8-10, 13, 15, 18-20, 35, 57-58, 60, 65

Melbourne Hospital	5, 13, 15, 18, 21-23, 29, 59, 62, 64, 70, 79, 81, 83, 98, 128, 139, 140, 162
Melbourne University	3, 4, 10, 14, 35, 55-56, 61-64, 67, 75, 80-82, 108, 141
Melbourne Women's Hospital	59-60
Mena House	99-100, 102-103, 105, 111, 115, 157
Mental asylums	65, 67, 70-71, 73-75
Meyer, Felix	1-4, 34, 59
Microbiome	86
Midwifery	59-60
Monash, General Sir John	126-127, 137, 141
M'Naghten Rules	32
Mullen, Dr William	32-33, 168
Munro-Ferguson, Lady Helen	108-110, 112, 124, 153
Murray, John (Chief Secretary)	70-74

N

National Council of Women	67-68
"Nature vs nurture"	29, 42, 61, 88, 90
Neild, James Edward	6, 8-10, 31, 58, 75
No 1 AGH	98, 101, 105-107, 118
No 2 AGH	98-100, 102, 108, 121
No 3 AGH Abbassia	121, 126

O

O'Hara, John	35, 57-58
Omama Gardens	see Joyous Gard.
Osler, Sir William	138

P

Paget, Sir James	92
Pasteurisation of milk	37-39
Pearce, The Hon. George	119, 143-145
Pensions	128, 134-135, 143, 146, 149
Physiotherapy	61-62, 108, 127, 157
Plunket Society nurses	152-153

Pre-Raphaelite Brotherhood	6
Pneumonia	101-102
Primrose, Sister Maude	151-152
Psychology	87, 139,142-143, 161, 189
Psychoanalysis	89, 142

R

Repatriation Department	128, 143, 146, 149, 150, 163
Roberts, Tom	3, 6, 12, 161
Rossetti, Dante Gabriel	6, 52
Royal College of Physicians	4, 13, 14, 19, 20, 22, 138
Royal Victorian Trained Nurses Association	see VTNA

S

Sewerage	25-26
Soil	33, 86
Springthorpe, Annie	see Inglis, Annie
Springthorpe, Daisie	see Johnstone, Daisie
Springthorpe, Dorothy Anne	12, 23, 53, 161
Springthorpe, Enid	12, 23, 46, 79, 98, 153, 162, 190
Springthorpe, Guy	46, 79, 80, 97, 98, 138, 140, 154, 162
Springthorpe, John (snr)	1, 64
Springthorpe, Lancelot	26, 46, 78, 79
St John Ambulance Association	8, 9, 75-78, 90, 160-161

T

Talbot Colony	see Epileptic Colony
Talbot, Lady Margaret	67-69
Tayler, Lloyd	8-9
Temperament	41, 87
Tennyson, Lord Alfred	6, 52
Tomb	see Cemetery Memorial
Tuberculin	30, 33, 36, 38, 168
Tuberculosis	25, 29-30, 34-39,44, 75, 86-87, 90, 161
Tucker, Professor	52
Tweddle, Joseph	151-153

V

Victorian Amateur Cycling Union	see Cycling
Victorian Trained Nurses Association (VTNA)	59-61, 64

W

"War's Awakening" play	160
Wesley College	2, 8, 161, 162
Weymouth Hospital	129, 131, 137
Williams, Sir William	76, 99, 106, 122, 156, 183
Women's Hospital	see Melbourne Women's Hospital

Y

Yorick Club	6-8, 162, 166

Shawline Publishing Group Pty Ltd
www.shawlinepublishing.com.au

SHAWLINE
PUBLISHING
GROUP